D0650650

Asheville-Buncombe
Technical Community College
Learning Resources Center
340 Victoria Road
Asheville, NC 28801

Discarded
Date   JUN 2 1 2023

Lucille's Car Care

Everything You Need to Know from Under the Hood—by America's Most Trusted Mechanic

Discarded
Date JUN 2 1 2023

Lucille Treganowan

with Gina Catanzarite

Asheville-Buncombe
Technical Community College
Learning Resources Center
340 Victoria Road
Asheville, NC 28801

HYPERION

NEW YORK

The Illustrations used in this book are of general and most common systems. Your car may have differences, so compare it. When in doubt, ask your favorite technician to go over it with you.

Illustrations by Vantage Art, Inc.

Copyright © 1996 ©WQED Pittsburgh and

Photographs on pp. 3 and 5 courtesy of Gerald B. Boyle.

All rights reserved. No part of this book may be used or reproduced in any manner whatsoever without the written permission of the Publisher. Printed in the United States of America. For information address: Hyperion, 114 Fifth Avenue, New York, New York 10011.

Library of Congress Cataloging-In-Publication Data

Treganowan, Lucille, 1930–
    Lucille's car care : everything you need to know from under the hood—by America's most trusted mechanic / Lucille Treganowan, with Gina Catanzarite.—1st. ed.
        p. cm.
    ISBN 0-7868-6201-7
        1. Automobiles—Maintenance and repair—Amateurs' manuals.
    2. Consumer protection—United States.   I. Catanzarite, Gina, 1965– .
    II. Title.
    TL152.T727   1996
    629.28'722—dc20   95–46041
                                                                CIP

Book Design by Richard Oriolo

FIRST EDITION

10 9 8 7 6 5 4 3 2 1

Acknowledgments

I extend my appreciation to the following people for technical discussions and for always being there for idea-bouncing: Gary Metz of Rosedale Technical Institute; Bill and Jim Kozub of Kozub Tune Up Center, and to Bill for being my editorial advisor; John Lucas of West Penn AAA; John Kubit of Action Auto Parts; Pete Klobucher of Transmissions by Lucille; and Mike Solito of Car Buying Consultants, Inc.

Also thanks to my son Kip for freeing my time, to my nephew Stanton for his ideas and research, and to my staff for making my life much easier during the book-writing process.

And to Gina Catanzarite for taking the time to understand how my mind works and for helping me to organize my thoughts in a way that looks good on paper.

Lucille Treganowan

My thanks to WQEX TV; WQED Pittsburgh; Home and Garden Television Network; and for his energy, support, and ability to get the ball rolling, Michael Fields.

I also extend immeasurable gratitude to my family, especially my parents, Pat and Libby Catanzarite; Paul and Selena Catanzarite; Tony Kauffman and my sister Christine Catanzarite, who might not have a driver's license but who has endless patience listening to me talk about cars.

And finally, for taking me along for the ride, my very sincere thanks to Lucille Treganowan, my favorite mechanic in "fifty-two states."

Gina Catanzarite

Contents

Contents

Contents

Lucille's Car Care

Introduction

It is difficult to recall just when I became an advocate for the education of car owners . . . but it's easy to recall when I first realized I wanted to learn about cars.

I was twenty-nine and working as a clerk at an automotive repair shop. The owner of the shop was a mechanic, not a businessman, and he left some pretty big holes as the company expanded. He was away from the shop a lot, and before long I found myself dealing with customers more than he did. I'd be standing on one side of the counter, facing a line of impatient customers on the other side. They'd all have questions and they'd all have car problems, but all I could say was, "I don't know. You'll have to wait. The owner will be back in a minute."

Needless to say, he usually did not come back in a minute, and I was left feeling like an absolute idiot, repeating, "I don't know. I don't know. I don't know."

So I decided to learn the terminology and started studying auto repair manuals. Don't get me wrong—there was no lightning bolt that struck me revealing my true vocation; this was simply a matter of personal pride because I didn't want to stand across from customers with a blank look on my face. My goal was to learn enough of the jargon to be able to talk intelligently to the customers.

In short, I wanted to learn just enough to fake it.

But then a strange thing happened: I became so fascinated with the miraculous operation of the automobile that I started studying for real. It wasn't easy, but I had ideal learning conditions. After all, I worked in an auto repair shop and had ample opportunity to observe and ask questions, even help out here and there. A whole new world opened up to me, and it wasn't long before this newfound interest in automobiles consumed my life.

Sure, there were some stumbling blocks along the way. There I was, a *woman* in 1963, offering my two cents' worth to a garage filled with men. Some of them ignored me, some took my advice, but mostly I felt like they were only humoring me—until I just happened to diagnose and repair a transmission that everyone else had given up for dead! You can bet they took me seriously after that.

Before long, we hired another woman to do the clerical work, and I handled customer intake, performed road testing, and became technical support for the mechanics. Not bad for someone who used to stand behind the counter saying, "I don't know. I don't know. I don't know."

Who would have guessed—way back in 1948 when I was just starting out—that this was where I would end up? I had come a long way from the teenager in Iola, Kansas (population 7,000), who dreamed of becoming an English teacher. During my sophomore year in college, I met and married a Pittsburgher, dropped out of college, and simply by chance took a clerical job in a Buick Agency while my husband finished college. Three children and nine years later it became apparent that my husband and I were not going to stay together.

Divorced and with the kids to support—and too proud to go home to Kansas with a failed marriage—I found myself wanting to return to college to try again for that English degree. Since the only thing on my

résumé was automotive clerical work, it looked like that was how I'd support my family and earn tuition.

It's a move that sealed my fate because that's what led me to the shop where I started out as the "clueless clerk."

It took five years to go from the clueless clerk to shop manager, but I was proud of what I had achieved—and my new love for auto repair made me pretty popular too. At parties, people were always coming up to me with their car questions, asking if another shop's repair quote sounded realistic, even wanting me to drive their cars to diagnose an impending problem.

Ruth Sherman, a friend who had watched me go from wife to mother to automotive buff with transmission fluid in my veins, suggested that I start holding classes to teach women the basics of automobiles. I taught my first "Powder Puff Mechanics" class at the local YMCA. Through the years, I continued teaching classes wherever I was asked. I guess that's when I really became an advocate for car owners, because I branched out to serve as a speaker for groups ranging from high school vocational programs to Kiwanis clubs, and would explain repair work in great detail to any interested customer who faced me across the counter.

After seven years of this, I became a partner in the company, and in another seven years I decided to open a shop of my own. The timing seemed perfect. My children were grown now, so I could afford to take the risk. Also, my male partners and I argued over just about everything.

I wanted a *new* approach to auto repair. I had a dream of a transmission shop that would offer great service and the highest quality work. The shop would be clean and orderly, and customers would leave to spread the word about our awe-inspiring levels of integrity and professionalism.

In the fall of 1973, I leased an abandoned gas station, got the first Small Business Administration loan ever given to a woman in western Pennsylvania, and christened my new shop Transmissions by Lucille.

As the old saying goes, the rest is history.

The business thrived, partly because I knew transmissions inside and out, partly because I was blessed with good luck, but always because I continued my crusade to help car owners be intelligent consumers. I'm still doing it today, and in this book you'll discover just what it takes to protect your investment and ensure a safer, smoother ride.

What you will *not* learn is how to become a professional auto technician. It is not my goal here to convert you to a new career, and if that's what you're looking for, you need manuals far more technical than this one. My goal with this book is to make you a smarter car consumer, to save you a trip to the shop now and then by teaching you to handle some basic repairs on your own, and to prove that with preventive maintenance you can keep small problems from becoming big problems and big problems from becoming even bigger expenses. I've also included consumer advice about choosing the right repair shop and buying a car, and a reference guide to help you identify symptoms when your car acts up. I suggest you read the book once all the way through and then keep it handy so you can refer to it for specific symptoms and repairs as they are needed.

Here's the bottom line: By understanding the operation of your car, you become a better, safer driver. You also save money by properly maintaining your car. And finally, *you* will be in control. Wouldn't it be great if, the next time you take your car to the shop, you go in armed with a little auto knowledge? That way you can discuss your car's needs with a technician, make intelligent decisions—and keep your name off the "sucker" list if someone tries to sell you parts or services you simply don't need!

Most repair shops are staffed by hardworking, honest people. I guarantee they'll appreciate a customer who understands the car's problem (I know I always do), and they'll bend over backward to give you great service.

Welcome to the world of grease and fumes. Trust me—you're going to love it!

Ladies and Gentlemen,
Start Your Engines

The first hurdle to get over in understanding your car is the fear that you could never possibly understand your car. I learned to drive when I was fourteen (delivering parts in an old Dodge truck for my father's plumbing business), and at the time it never would have occurred to me to learn anything more than how to turn the key and start the car. The whole process just seemed so huge, so miraculous, so incomprehensible. But let's face facts: Popcorn can seem miraculous too, until you understand how it works.

The key is to separate the different systems, learn their components, and then learn how each one operates. With a clear understanding of the functions and relationship of all the systems, understanding your car is simply a matter of logic.

Okay, let's take the popcorn analogy one step further. How amazing, how incredible, that a tiny kernel of corn can suddenly transform into a little white fluff of snack food. Of course, it's not so amazing if you know there's a tiny drop of moisture inside that kernel, and when you drop the kernel into hot oil the moisture heats, then turns to steam, and the steam causes the kernel to explode. Knowing this, you would never drop corn kernels into cold oil and expect them to pop.

It's the same way with your car: When you know the correct process, you'll be less likely to do the wrong thing.

Imagine this: You're blocking an intersection, car stalled, engine flooded. Even though you faintly recall your high school driver's ed teacher saying something about not pumping the gas pedal, you hear a horn honk behind you . . .

Then another . . .

And another . . .

And the next thing you know you're pumping at that gas pedal desperately, frantically hoping your car will start and those people will stop scowling and that everyone will just lay off the horns.

But how would you handle the situation if you understood what flooding really means? The engine is not starting because the spark plugs are wet. Why? Because through some malfunction or driver error, liquid gasoline got into the cylinders instead of gas vapor. Armed with this knowledge, you have the confidence to sit back, relax, and tough it out. Let the maniacs honk and scream and make obscene gestures. You, the Educated Auto Owner, know that you have to wait for the gasoline to evaporate and that pumping the gas pedal will only prolong your problem.

It's all part of a simple, logical process.

So before I take you into the complexities of fixing your car when it's broken, how about we go through a brief lesson in how the car works in the first place? That way, instead of being angry and frustrated when your car malfunctions, you can be appreciative and admiring when it gives you tremendous performance on the road.

Chapters Two and Seven also make a handy little reference guide if your auto technician likes to inundate you with a lot of jargon and technical explanations. Just flip to the page explaining how that system works, and then you and your mechanic are back on an even playing field.

I try to explain things in a very simple, straightforward way, but some of you who are new to the world of auto mechanics might panic when you hear technical-sounding names like *positive crankcase ventilation valve* or *constant velocity joints*, so you might want to reread some of the sections if that's what it takes for you to get a clear picture in your head. As I told you before, the first hurdle is getting over your fear of understanding this stuff, so take a deep breath, summon your self-confidence, and go for it. Learning about cars really is no more difficult than learning the art of gourmet cooking or studying a foreign language. It might take a little work and a lot of concentration, but it's certainly not impossible.

I guarantee one thing: You'll truly respect the automobile once you are exposed to everything that must happen between turning the key and moving the car.

Pistons and Spark Plugs
and Belts, Oh My!

id you ever sing the song "Dry Bones" when you were little? You know, "The foot bone's connected to the shin bone / The shin bone's connected to the knee bone / The knee bone's connected to the thigh bone," and so on.

Well, there are a lot of connecting parts inside your automobile too, and turning the key in the ignition sets the whole process in motion.

First of all, let's just take a look at the word "ignition." The root word, "ignite," describes exactly what happens when you start the car: An electrical spark from the spark plug ignites a mixture of gasoline and air in each of the car's *cylinders*. Cylinders are simply combustion chambers, the places where this ignition takes place. After ignition, the burning gas vapors expand, and that expansion forces down a *piston*.

If you're more comfortable in the kitchen then you are in a garage, let me use an analogy to make this clearer. Have you ever used a cake decorating device? You push in a lever to force icing out of the container. The icing would be gas vapor, the container is like a cylinder, and the lever pushing out the icing is like the piston.

Each piston is joined by a connecting rod to the *crankshaft,* which is a large, heavy, strangely shaped shaft. One by one, in special order, each piston goes up and down, doing its part to turn the crankshaft. (Think about how a row of horses goes up and down on a merry-go-round.) The *torque* (another word to describe power) produced by this turning crankshaft is then harnessed to operate everything else in the car. Using belts, it produces electricity by way of the *alternator,* operates the power steering pump, and runs the air conditioner.

Now I'm going to give you a short explanation of how each of the seven systems operates in your car. *Don't skip this section.* It's kind of like the eager kid who wants to jump into the pool before he's actually learned how to swim. You can't dive under the hood of a car and expect to fix things unless you understand how they're supposed to work in the first place. We're talking about learning the logical process, and in a car this is where it all begins:

the power train

the electrical system

the fuel system

the exhaust system

the brake system

the steering system

the suspension system

The Power Train

The *power train* is the name given to the engine, transmission, driveshaft, and rear axle assembly. It literally is a "train" of components carrying power from one end of the car to the other.

The power train system

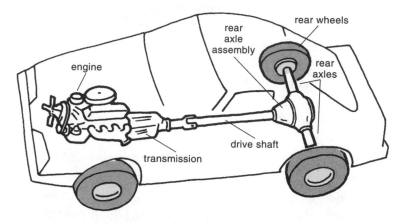

In older, conventional rear-wheel-drive vehicles, the engine is in front and the transmission is directly behind it. A long driveshaft, with *universal joints* (sometimes called *U joints*) at each end for flexibility, connects the transmission to the rear axle assembly (or simply, the "rear end"), and from there axles connect to the rear wheels.

In the transmission, the power from the engine is being adapted to the kind of road on which you are driving and to the amount of weight (load) in your car. (This is referred to as *road and load conditions*.) Once the transmission adapts to road and load conditions, it carries power through the driveshaft to the rear end, and then the power changes direction and goes to the rear wheels.

Let's take a closer look at the components in the power train.

The Engine

The engine is the sole source of power for your car. This power is in the form of torque, which is defined literally as "twist force" produced by the turning crankshaft. The engine also supplies hot water for the heater, and it creates tremendous vacuum—the force that operates power brakes and all sorts of accessories. The crankshaft uses various belts to drive the air conditioner, a water pump for cooling the engine, a

Power Play

I 've explained the power train in conventional rear-wheel-drive vehicles, but power trains can be arranged in a few different ways, based on the model of your car. You can consult your car's manual for a diagram of its power train, but I'll help you out with some simple definitions here.

✔ In *front-wheel-drive* cars, both the engine and the transmission are up front under the hood, usually side by side. The rear-axle assembly, which in front-wheel-drive vehicles becomes the *final drive,* may be bolted either to the side of the transmission or inside the same case with the transmission. The latter is more common and is known as a *transaxle.*

The front axles serve as driveshafts that carry the power from the final drive to the front wheels. The front-wheel-drive axles also must have joints on each end for flexibility, and they use a special kind of U joint called *constant velocity joints* (or *CV joints*), covered by black, accordion-like boots to retain lubrication.

Front-wheel-drive vehicles now outnumber rear-wheel-drive, and every year their numbers increase.

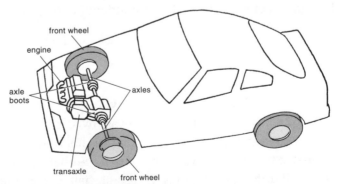

The power train in front-wheel-drive, and, opposite, four-wheel-drive-vehicles

✔ *Four-wheel-drive* vehicles have the engine up front, transmission directly behind it, and a transfer case bolted to the transmission. From the transfer case, one driveshaft carries power to the front wheels and another driveshaft carries power to the rear wheels. Four-wheel-drive vehicles may operate like this all the time, but most later-model vehicles give the driver the option to use either two or four wheels.

✔ These days manufacturers also offer something called *all-wheel drive,* with a little unit bolted inside the transmission pan or on the side of the transmission. It's similar to four-wheel-drive since it has the ability to send power to all the wheels, but it's not as sturdy as the four-wheel-drive unit found in sport-utility vehicles and trucks, which is housed in a separate transfer case connected to the rear of the transmission and designed especially for heavy-duty service. (In fact, the first four-wheel-drive vehicle was the army Jeep of World War II.) All-wheel drive is designed for snow-covered roads and is available mostly on passenger cars and vans.

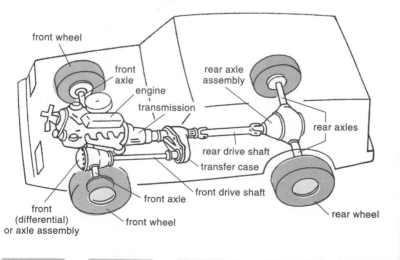

front wheel

front axle

engine

transmission

rear axle assembly

rear axles

rear drive shaft

transfer case

front drive shaft

front axle

front wheel

front (differential) or axle assembly

rear wheel

power steering pump, and an alternator for generating electricity.

How much power your car produces is determined by three things: the number of cylinders in the engine, the type of fuel system, and the *compression ratio*. (The more compressed the gas vapor, the more power it will produce when ignited.)

Early-model cars have engines with cylinders in a straight line, as do many of today's little four-cylinder compact cars. Most later-model cars have cylinders arranged in the shape of a V, which takes up less space but is still capable of producing more power. You've probably heard of V-6 or V-8 engines, which refer to both the V configuration and the number of cylinders in the car. Believe it or not, Jaguar actually makes a V-12 engine. Imagine how much power you'd get out of a car like that!

NOTE: *Diesel engines* operate very much the same as gasoline engines, with pistons turning a crankshaft. The difference is that diesel engines use the less refined and less expensive diesel fuel instead of gasoline, and the diesel fuel's vapor is ignited by intense heat in the compression chamber, *not* by spark plugs.

The Transmission

I mentioned earlier that the *transmission* adapts engine power to road and load conditions. In other words, it determines how much power your car needs and then supplies the necessary amount by shifting to various gears. An object as heavy as an automobile needs a lot of power to move it from a dead stop, but once it's in motion it requires less power to keep it going. Think back to your high school physics class and you'll realize this is simply Newton's Law of Motion: A body at rest tends to remain at rest, and a body in motion tends to remain in motion, until acted upon by an outside force.

Your car may have either a *manual transmission* (sometimes called a *standard transmission*) or an *automatic transmission*. With a manual transmission, the car's *driver* has to decide which gear to be in and then use the clutch to physically move one gear to mesh with another. With an automatic transmission, the car's *transmission* does the deciding and puts the car in that gear on its own.

If you didn't need to move at more than one slow speed, and you never had to back up, you wouldn't even need a transmission. In fact, in some warehouses they use vehicles that don't have transmissions; they simply drive at low speed and turn around by going in circles.

The Driveshaft

The driveshaft connects the transmission to the rear axle assembly. If the driveshaft were one long, solid shaft, it would suffer a lot of stress going over bumps and around bends. So universal joints are placed on each end of the shaft to allow motion both sideways and up and down. (Remember, in front-wheel-drive cars the front axles serve as driveshafts and have CV joints in them.)

The Rear Axle Assembly

After the transmission picks up the power and adapts it to the car's needs, the power goes to the rear axle assembly or, in front-wheel-drive cars, the *final drive*. Up until now, the torque is transmitted in a straight line from the rear of the crankshaft in the engine. Once the torque gets to the rear end, or final drive, it goes through a series of gears that change its direction and take it to the wheels. Which wheels the power goes to, front or back, depends on whether you have a front-wheel-drive car or a rear-wheel-drive car. Four-wheel-drive vehicles send power to all four wheels.

The Electrical System

T here are eight little words any repair person can utter that I assure you strike terror in the hearts of car owners everywhere: *The problem could be in the electrical system.*

I've found over the years that if people are intimidated by understanding auto mechanics, then the very notion of understanding electrical components sends them into a cold sweat. To that end, I have both good news and bad news about your car's electrical system. The good news is, some components of the car's electrical system are actually very, very simple. And the bad news is . . . some are not.

Let's go with the simple stuff first and work our way up.

Lights and Accessories

There is nothing complicated about the electrical parts of the lights and accessories in your car. They are controlled simply by on-off switches, just like any appliance you have in your house. Whether you pull a knob, push a button, or flick a switch, you're doing exactly the same thing you'd do to turn on the lights in your bedroom or flick on the coffee grinder in your kitchen.

Your car also has a fuse box similar to the one in your home, where fuses are used to protect the wiring from damage caused by a component failure. If you own a very early model car, you're fortunate enough to have a simple and accessible fuse box, which makes changing a fuse a do-it-yourself task. Not so in later-model cars, which often have multiple fuse boxes, hard-to-identify parts, and tricky replacement requirements. Because you could inadvertently cause a lot of damage, I advise you to leave fuse replacement to the experts.

The Battery

Most people have jumped a dead battery using jumper cables. Those of you who have not jumped a battery have probably at least seen it being done. And anyone who neither has jumped a battery nor seen one being jumped is the person most likely to leave his or her headlights on in the parking lot.

The battery has two roles in the electrical system: It stores electricity so there is energy available when it's time to start the car, and it operates the lights and accessories when your engine is not running.

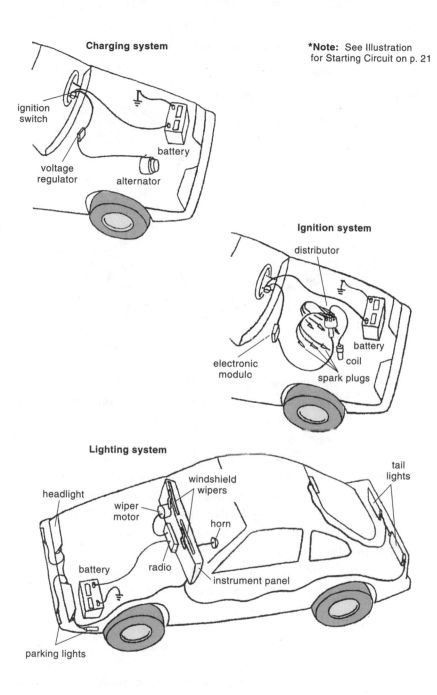

Charging system

ignition switch

voltage regulator

alternator

battery

*Note: See Illustration for Starting Circuit on p. 21

Ignition system

distributor

electronic module

spark plugs

coil

battery

Lighting system

headlight

wiper motor

windshield wipers

horn

tail lights

battery

radio

instrument panel

parking lights

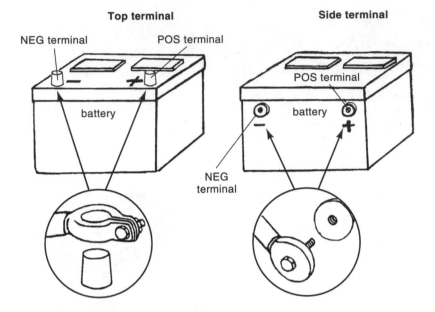

Two types of batteries

Top terminal

Side terminal

NEG terminal

POS terminal

POS terminal

battery

battery

NEG terminal

Once the car engine is running, the battery is no longer the source of electricity. The *alternator* takes over and produces electricity for the car and also recharges the battery—although the battery is always standing by, ready to supply additional electrical current whenever you need it. (By the way, if your car is a relic or, more politely, a "classic" car, a generator will supply electricity instead of an alternator.)

There are two terminals on your car's battery—one positive and one negative—and they are located on either the battery's top or its side. A cable connects the positive terminal to the car's starting circuit and other electrical systems; the negative terminal is connected by cable to a *ground,* usually the engine block. The ground completes an electrical circuit and makes it possible for the current to flow.

The Starting Circuit

Have you ever seen a really old movie where the driver starts his vehicle by turning a crank at the front of the car? That crank was actually a

Starting circuit

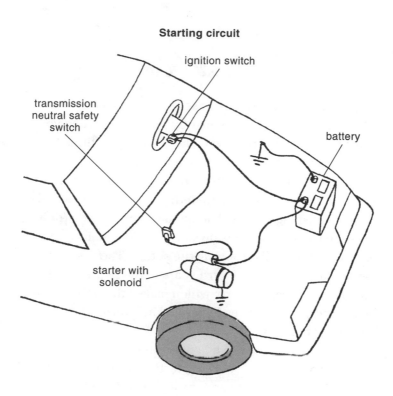

tool inserted in the front of the crankshaft, which has to turn in order to start the car, and in the old days drivers had to do it by hand. Those old-fashioned cranks were responsible for a lot of injuries, and thankfully they were replaced with electric motors. I guess you might call this the first luxury feature on an automobile, because it really was the first innovation to make the car more user-friendly.

Think about what happens when you first turn the key in the ignition switch of your car. In the first position the lights come on, but they're being powered by the battery because the engine isn't running at that point. Once you turn the key farther, the battery powers a switch that activates the *starter* (a round, cylinderlike electrical motor with a gear on the end). The starter gear meshes with a *flywheel*, another gear attached to the crankshaft, and rotates fast enough to start the engine.

Manual Labor

As you may know, it is possible to start a car with a manual transmission just by pushing it. When you start the car the normal way, the starter gear turns the crankshaft, which starts the engine, which turns gears in the transmission, which turns the driveshaft, which turns gears in the rear end, and then the axles turn the wheels.

By pushing a car with a manual transmission (or a pre–1960 automatic transmission), you're eliminating the starter and actually *reversing* the action: The wheels turn, which turn axles, which turn gears in the rear end, which makes the driveshaft turn, which makes the transmission gears turn, which makes the crankshaft turn, which then starts the engine.

I've known people who have gone for *months* with a bad battery or starter, always starting the car by pushing or drifting it. But what happens if you get caught in a situation where you can't push the car, as when two cars block you in? In a case like that, you're stuck. Even though this little trick won't do any harm to the car, you'd have to be a real gambler to rely on it for long.

The Charging Circuit

With the great need for electrical energy in today's cars, there has to be a really good source of power. But the battery can store only so much energy, and once it's used up, the battery is ineffective. That's why cars come equipped with *alternators*. The alternator produces electrical current, but since a belt connects it to the crankshaft, it will generate electricity only when the engine is running.

The alternator is controlled by a *voltage regulator.* It tells the alternator when to produce more energy and when to produce less energy, depending on how much electrical equipment is running. The alternator also recharges the battery after it's drained from starting the car. Ideally, the voltage regulator will keep the energy output just high enough to meet the car's needs, but if it can't do that the battery makes up the difference.

The Ignition System

The ignition system delivers a high-voltage spark to each spark plug, which then ignites gas vapor in the combustion chamber. Just to give you an idea of how much of a spark we're talking about here, the process *begins* with approximately 12 volts of electricity from the battery when you turn the key—and that's so low you can't even feel it if you touch it. Once the engine is running and the spark reaches the spark plugs, those 12 volts have increased to at least 10,000 and up to 30,000 volts, depending on the type of ignition system.

If knowing that has you afraid even to open your hood, let alone start handling things under there, don't worry. The hot spark will be there only when the engine is running, and voltage alone isn't what hurts you. Voltage refers to the pressure that causes a current to move, but the actual strength of the current lies in the amperage. It *is* possible to get a shock, but risk is minimal because while the volts are high, the amperage is actually quite low.

The Fuel System

E veryone knows liquid gasoline goes into the tank of a car. But it remains liquid only for storage because, in order to start the car, liquid gas has to become a vapor. The fuel system of your car is responsible for storing fuel, transporting it to the combustion area, and turning liquid gasoline into gas vapor.

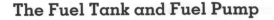

The Fuel Tank and Fuel Pump

The fuel tank stores the liquid gasoline and has a float—connected to a gauge on your dash—that reports how much gas you have in the tank.

The fuel pump transfers liquid gasoline from the tank through fuel lines and a fuel filter and takes it to the engine area where it is mixed with air. Once the liquid fuel reaches the engine area, the mixing process takes place in either a *carburetor*, a *fuel-injection system*, or the *intake manifold*, depending on the type of car you have.

The Carburetor

The carburetor was the fuel-mixer of choice for many years. Check your owner's manual to see if you have a carburetor or fuel injection.

Carbureted fuel system

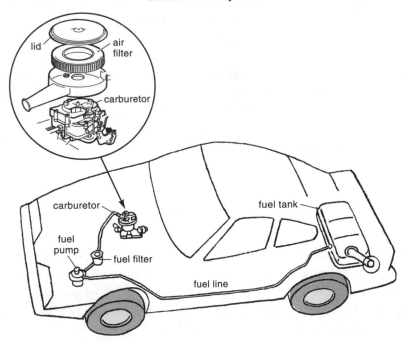

Fuel Mixtures

Your car requires a richer fuel/air mixture in two circumstances. The first is when your car engine is cold. When it's cold a little lid (called a *choke butterfly*) on top of the carburetor closes so the car gets only a little more gasoline but a lot less air. As the engine warms up, this little lid will open again and conditions return to normal.

Sometimes, on a cold day, the choke fails to close on its own and your engine won't start. If you're looking for a good way to impress your friends, simply remove the air cleaner on top of the carburetor and pop the choke butterfly shut.

The other time your car requires a richer mixture of fuel and air is when it needs a spurt of power. When you step on the gas pedal, an accelerator pump in the carburetor adds a squirt of gasoline and only a little more air, so the mixture is richer.

In cars that have fuel-injection systems instead of carburetors, the system uses sensors and other sophisticated equipment to enrich the gas-air mixture or to lean it out.

Under the air filter lid, sitting in the middle of the engine, you may have either kind of fuel system.

The carburetor will mix fuel and air together in the proper proportions: fifteen parts air to one part gasoline. That's measured by weight, so you can imagine that's quite a lot of air! But where does it all come from? It's drawn in from the outside and passes through an air filter, where dirt is trapped. The clean air travels down through the carburetor, where rushing air mixes with the liquid gasoline, and the result is vapor that travels to the combustion chamber.

The Fuel-Injection System

Fuel-injection systems date back to 1957, when they were installed in some General Motors cars, but they weren't used commonly until the development of computer controls in the 1980s. Without the computer controls, fuel injection was crude, unreliable, and expensive to boot.

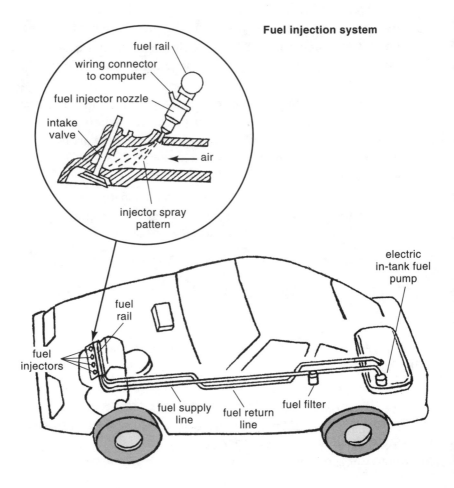

Fuel injection system

With today's fuel-injection systems, the mixing process of gasoline and air actually takes place right in the combustion chamber, or in an *intake manifold* (a series of passages that go into the combustion chamber). Injector valves shoot the fuel in to mix with a constant flow of air, which is brought in through tubes directed to each cylinder. The goal is to achieve the optimum fuel/air ratio that gives the best gas mileage and the most power.

The whole process works kind of like a garden hose. If you have a garden hose with a good nozzle, you are able to adjust the flow of water lower and lower until what you actually get is a strong spray of mist. What you get in a car is a strong spray of gas mist.

There is no end to the sophisticated systems that control fuel injection on late-model cars. They can feed fuel in a continuous flow or in a pulsed, timed manner. Computers feed information about speed, temperature, and air pressure both inside and outside the intake manifold, and the injectors will deliver more or less fuel based on what the computer directs. In fact, credit any advances in engine power in the last few years to the innovative designs of fuel injection systems.

The Exhaust System

From time to time, I get a customer who thinks the tailpipe, muffler, and exhaust pipe are all the same thing when actually they are separate parts of the *exhaust system*. This system removes the burned gas vapor from the engine so a backup of exhaust gases won't bog down engine power.

Unfortunately, those exhaust gases not only affect the engine performance, they are harmful to people and to the environment as well. It's not just an annoyance to listen to the loud roar of a leaking exhaust system, there's the danger of being subjected to odorless, colorless, deadly carbon monoxide. And in urban areas, at least half of the air pollutants that become smog are caused by gasoline-powered vehicles.

When I talk about an exhaust system, it would be difficult to ignore *emissions,* since the two are so closely related. That's why I'm including explanations of both of them here.

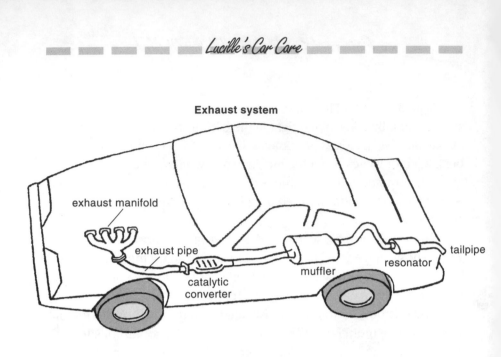

Exhaust system

The Exhaust Manifold

Exhaust leaves the cylinders after combustion has taken place and then goes to the exhaust manifold, which is a system of passages leading from each cylinder to the exhaust pipe.

The Catalytic Converter

The catalytic converter is part of the emissions system, and a car can have one of two kinds. The first is similar to a flat, covered bowl full of pellets. The other is tubular with a honeycomb inside. Any unburned gas vapor will be chemically changed here to cut down additional discharge of pollutants from the tailpipe.

The exhaust pipe bolts to the exhaust manifold at the rear of the engine and connects to the catalytic converter by way of a short pipe. Exhaust gases pass through the catalytic converter and travel through another pipe to the muffler.

In addition to the catalytic converter, car engines are also equipped with a *positive crankcase ventilation valve* (PCV) and an *exhaust gas recirculation valve* (EGR), which work toward reducing air pollution.

Catalytic converters

Honeycomb type

Pellet type

inlet

honeycomb

inlet

shell

pellets

shell

outlet

heat shield

outlet

The Muffler

The exhaust gases traveling from the catalytic converter end up in the muffler. Here, the roar of the engine is muffled, and the gases continues to pass into the tailpipe and out the rear of the car.

On some cars, especially larger luxury models, a second smaller muffler, called a *resonator,* quiets the sound even more. The resonator usually is positioned behind the muffler and in front of the tailpipe.

The Brake System

When you were a kid, did you ever pedal your bicycle to the top of a steep hill and then, in a tremendous show of bravado, take a wild ride to the bottom? You might have enjoyed it when you *started,* but I'm guessing somewhere in the middle of the ride you realized, *It would be nice if I knew how to stop this thing—preferably in a way that doesn't involve slamming into a wall.* (My sons skinned their knees and elbows many times before learning this lesson.)

Even though the years have passed and you might have traded your

Schwinn for a Chevy, things haven't changed. It is infinitely more important to know how to *stop* a car than it is to get one to move. How the brakes work is just as important as how *you* work the brakes, so let's take a look at the components and proper driving techniques to save wear and tear.

Your car will have one of two types of brakes: *disc brakes* or *drum brakes*. Disc brakes stop quicker and run cooler, and the trend in later-model cars has been toward disc brakes. Any car manufactured in the last decade should have at least a combination of both kinds, with disc brakes on the front wheels and drum brakes on the rear. Check the owner's manual if you aren't sure which kind are on your car.

Drum Brakes

In drum brakes, the component is shaped like a rather short, stocky cylinder that fits over the *brake shoes*. (Brake shoes are curved plates with a veneer lining of friction material.) Drum brakes are hydraulically operated, which means they are controlled by fluid under pressure. When you step on the brake pedal, fluid is forced from the master cylinder through a series of connections to small cylinders in each of the wheels. The pressure from the cylinder forces the brake shoes against the surface of the brake drum, and depending on how hard you hit the brakes, the car either slows down or stops. When you ease up on the brake pedal, springs pull the brake shoes away from the drum, and the wheels can turn again.

Disc Brakes

In this type of brake a disc—or *rotor,* as it is commonly called—is attached to each wheel, and on top of each one is a caliper, which grabs the rotor with pads lined with friction material and stops it each time you apply the brakes.

As an example, let's go back to the bicycle we talked about earlier. When you were a kid, did you ever turn a bicycle upside down and

Drum brake construction

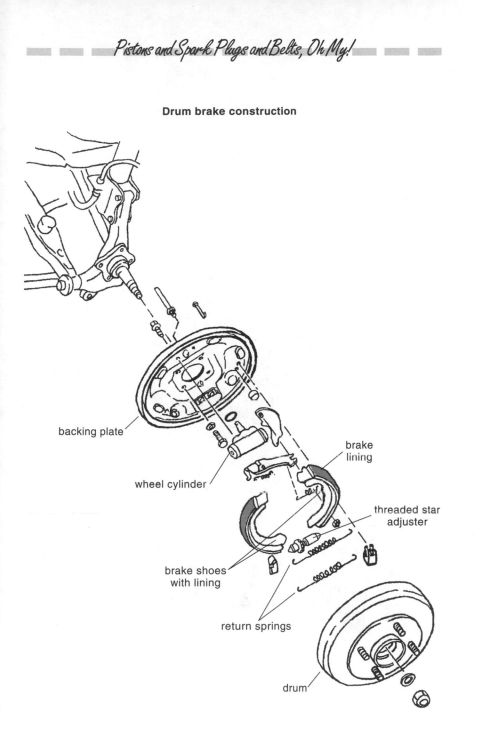

backing plate

wheel cylinder

brake shoes with lining

brake lining

threaded star adjuster

return springs

drum

Disc brake construction

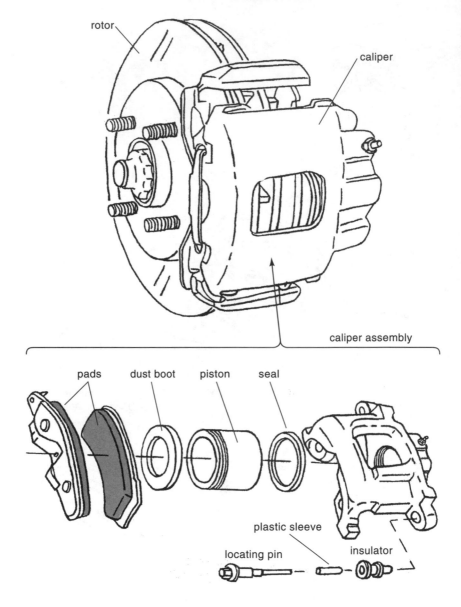

An Ounce of Prevention

B *rake failure* is a common fear of drivers. In fact, one national survey even named it as the number-one fear. In spite of that, the National Car Care Council reports that nearly one-third of all cars on the road today have brakes in need of repair.

You can avoid brake failure by simply maintaining your brakes according to your owner's manual and practicing proper brake application to save wear and tear. If you still fear a complete loss of brakes, rest assured it's not very likely to happen. Either the front and rear brakes are on separate hydraulic systems, or the left and right sides are on separate hydraulic systems; odds are slim that both systems will fail at the same time.

spin the wheels really fast? If you grabbed the wheel with your hand, you'd be stopping the wheel the same way a caliper grabs the rotor to stop it.

In fact, this is a good analogy to use in talking about brake wear and tear too. Imagine you are wearing a leather glove when you grab that spinning bicycle wheel. If you grab the wheel while it's turning at a high speed and stop it immediately, that glove will get scuffed and wear out pretty quickly.

But if you *gradually* slow the wheel by gently touching it several times, the glove remains cooler and lasts much longer. It's exactly the same case with brake lining, which is why you should *pump* the brakes gently in anticipation of a stop; don't slam them to the floor. Keep in mind, also, that the front brakes do from 60 to 80 percent of the braking, so brake lining on front and rear wheels wears out at different rates.

The Parking Brake

To be honest, I hate the term "parking brake" for the device that keeps the vehicle from rolling when it's parked. It's too easy to confuse that with the "park" position in your automatic transmission.

Some people refer to it as the "hand brake," but I don't like that either; in many cars, these brakes are actually applied with your foot.

How about "emergency brake"? That's definitely no good, because it is *not* designed for emergencies; it's designed to keep cars from rolling once they are parked.

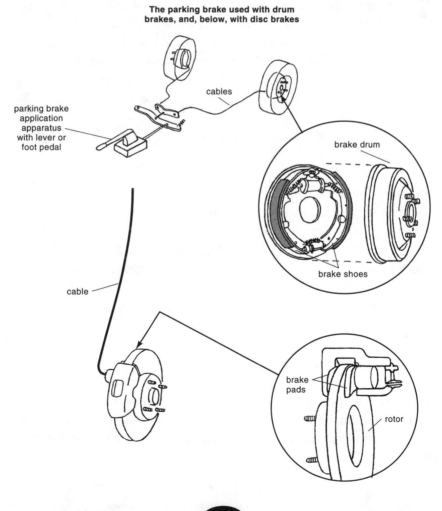

The parking brake used with drum brakes, and, below, with disc brakes

cables

parking brake application apparatus with lever or foot pedal

brake drum

brake shoes

cable

brake pads

rotor

Okay, so we're back to calling it the "parking brake."

This brake is *not* hydraulic, it's mechanical. Two cables go from the lever or pedal (depending on whether you apply yours by hand or by foot) to the rear wheels. In drum brakes, the cables pull the brake shoes tightly against the drum. In disc brakes, cables pull the pads tightly to the rotor. Both keep the car from moving when it's parked.

One important tip about parking brakes: I definitely recommend that you use yours on a regular basis. People who live in cold climates seem to be afraid the parking brake will freeze, and while that is possible, it's also pretty rare. Other people just don't want to bother with parking brakes. But the fact is, if you don't use it regularly, the cables may rust and seize and then you won't be able to use it at all.

Power Brakes

Stopping a big, heavy car requires a lot of strength, and the faster the car is going, the more strength it takes. Most larger cars come equipped with power brakes to make the process easier for the driver. As soon as you press down on the brake pedal, the *power booster* is activated, and it assists you in applying the brakes. Power boosters get their power from engine vacuum, so if the engine isn't running—for instance, if your car stalls—you're going to experience a problem. A reserve will give you a power assist for two or three stops, but after that your power brakes desert you.

ABS Brakes

Think back to your first driving lesson. More than likely someone sat in the passenger seat yelling "Pump the brakes! Pump the brakes!" You probably spent some time jerking the car around but eventually mastered the art of the smooth stop.

Now think back to the first time you were driving along and a dog ran in front of your car . . . or a child's ball rolled into the street, or some truck jumped the red light, or a deer leaped out of nowhere onto the highway. Those are all pretty scary situations, and your first impulse was probably to slam on the brakes. If you followed that impulse, you found out that the result was brakes that locked and a car that went into a frightening skid.

Antilock brake systems, or ABS brakes, were designed to ward off this kind of disaster. With ABS brakes, you are *supposed* to slam on the brakes in an emergency situation. A computer controls each wheel individually and takes over to pump the brakes on its own (much faster than any human could). That helps to stabilize the car and in most situations reduces the stopping distance.

The jury is still out, however, on the value of ABS brakes. Many critics claim that statistics show no reduction in the number of collisions since ABS brakes were first introduced. One problem may be that people tend to drive *less* safely if the car has ABS brakes, because they expect that brake system to work miracles.

Don't lapse into dangerous habits because your car has an added safety feature. In the same way that car air bags are most effective when used in conjunction with a seat belt, ABS brakes are most effective when used by a conscientious driver.

The Steering System

Years ago back in Kansas, my two brothers and I used to make go-carts in the driveway. An orange crate made up the body, and a rod with wheels on each end would be attached in the back. Attaching the front wheels was more of a challenge because we had to be able to steer the cart.

The solution was to put a wheel on each end of a narrow board, loosely connect that board to the front center of the orange crate, and then tie on a rope. The rope acted just like the reins on a horse. If you want the horse to turn left, pull on the left side of the reins. If you want the horse to turn right, pull on the right side.

This go-cart technology was the most rudimentary steering system, and believe it or not, it is the same principle behind the steering systems in today's most sophisticated cars.

The components of the steering system

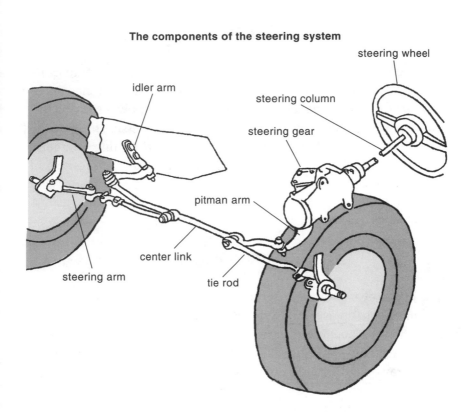

Steering Linkage

The steering wheel on your car is attached, by means of a shaft, to the *steering linkage* connecting both front wheels. But unlike the old wooden board on the go-cart, this steering linkage is not a straight shaft; it's a series of rods, arms, and joints that allow each wheel to operate independently. If your front wheels were connected, as in the old go-carts, what would happen when you turn? Steer to the left, and the left wheel would turn only a very short distance, but the right wheel would have to swing out much farther. You'd literally be dragging the right wheel, and that's no good at all.

Power Steering

Like the brakes on your car, operating the steering wheel manually requires a lot of strength and effort. By means of a belt, the crankshaft drives the *power steering pump* on a car equipped with a power steering feature. The pump sends power steering fluid through pressure hoses to the steering gear box, and this hydraulic force assists in steering your car.

With a good power steering system and an adequate reserve of power steering fluid, you should be able to complete a smooth turn with very little effort.

The Suspension System

Did you ever enter a curve too fast and find that your car felt as if it just might tip over on two wheels? The reason you don't lose control of the car is because of *shocks and struts*, which aid in the car's ability to cling to the road. Shocks and struts also help keep you in control if you stray onto the road's bumpy shoulder.

Various types of springs, most commonly *leaf springs* and *coil springs*, help soften the bumps and keep the vehicle level. But a car's suspension system is not there just to make the ride smoother. It provides optimum tire wear and better handling of the car by working in conjunction with the steering system. In fact, some automotive experts consider the steering and the suspension to be parts of one system.

Let's continue to use our homemade go-cart as an example of automotive engineering. Something was completely missing from those old go-carts: comfort and stability. In a go-cart that's half the fun, but think about how you'd feel at the end of a long car trip if your body, instead of the suspension system, took the brunt of the bumps.

Shock Absorbers

Shock absorbers, located near each wheel, do exactly what their name implies. There are various types—some filled with fluid, others filled

Shock absorber construction

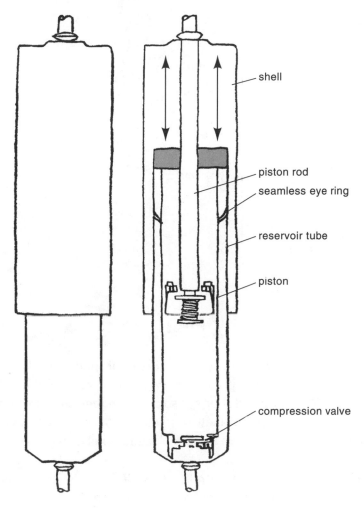

shell

piston rod

seamless eye ring

reservoir tube

piston

compression valve

with compressed gas—but they all serve the same function. After hitting a bump, a vehicle has a tendency to continue bouncing up and down because springs in the suspension system have no means to stop the motion quickly. Shock absorbers control the springs by allowing one good bounce, then absorbing the shock so the car can return to its normal level.

Strut construction

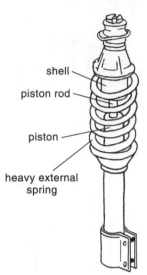

shell

piston rod

piston

heavy external
spring

Struts

Most later-model cars now use struts instead of shocks. Struts are like shock absorbers, but the springs are already built in. They're a definite improvement over the old shock absorbers, but they are also more expensive to replace. Unfortunately, neither shocks nor struts can be fixed; the components have to be replaced entirely, so it's wise to invest in quality the first time.

Heavy-duty shocks and struts are available for vehicles that are heavily loaded, mostly commercial trucks and vans.

From top to bottom, front to back, we've covered the systems that make up your automobile. And now that you know the basics, now that you understand the logical process that keeps your car on the road, we're going to move on to the really fun stuff. Pull out your tools and head for the open road, because from regular maintenance to simple repairs, *you* are going to be one impressive car care customer.

3

The Scouting Trip:

Don't Leave Home Without It

ost homeowners protect their investment by setting aside time each week to clean the house, inspect it for problems, and make a plan for repairs. A car is a huge investment too, but few people allot the same kind of time and attention to it. I suggest you schedule a regular *scouting trip* to assess the condition of your car and tackle small repair and maintenance tasks, since a little diligence and upkeep will extend the car's life and make it an exceptional value at trade-in time. A scouting trip is also a good way to gain confidence, not just in your car but also in your own abilities as its owner and driver. Just as you assign household chores to your children, be sure to include all of your family's drivers in the scouting trip responsibilities.

Scouting trips don't take much time. Mark them on your calendar once a month and block out about an hour and a half. I like to do them on Saturday morning or during a leisurely Sunday afternoon. The truth is I really enjoy this time tinkering with my car, and I like to do it when I'm not rushed or likely to be interrupted.

Find a safe location for your scouting trip. A private driveway or garage is ideal, but if you don't have that luxury, find a safe spot on a quiet street. If your street sees frequent traffic, don't risk it. Instead, I recommend you take the car to a safe, level parking lot of a shopping center during off-peak hours.

Finally, start a Car Care Binder to record data. Use it to record dates and types of services performed on the car; store receipts from services and parts; and keep a calendar reminding you of change intervals for fluids, tire rotation, and state inspections. This binder is exceptionally valuable if you decide to sell the car too, because future owners will be ecstatic to own such detailed maintenance records.

In a separate section of your Car Care Binder, enter the results of each of your scouting trips. Make three lists as you go:

1. Small repairs

2. Maintenance to prevent problems

3. Stuff for the repair shop

Supplies for your first scouting trip might require a trip to the auto parts store to purchase some cleaning agents and a few tools. If you buy everything on the list, expect to invest between $300 and $400. Considering the average car has a price tag around $20,000, this seems like a modest amount to pay for upkeep. If you're looking to cut costs until you commit yourself totally to becoming a real amateur mechanic, hold off from buying the floor jack and jack stands, because they'll run you about $250.

The Car Care Shopping List

✔ Tool kit—includes a full range of sizes in wrenches, sockets with a ratchet handle, and an assortment of screwdrivers with both standard and Phillips heads. For newer cars you will also need an assortment of torx bits with a screwdriver handle.

✔ Trouble light—equipped with a shield, hanging hook, and a long cord

✔ Rubber mallet or hammer

✔ Floor jack and jack stands (*Never* work on a car jacked up with the jack designed for changing flat tires.)

✔ Cleaning agents designed for your car's interior and exterior

✔ Tire gauge

✔ Battery cable terminal puller

✔ Battery terminal cleaning tool

✔ Flat pan for catching oil or antifreeze

✔ Spark plug socket—including ratchet handle and feeler gauge

✔ Antifreeze tester

✔ Four-way tire wrench

You'll certainly acquire tools, cleaning agents, and repair products as you get more familiar with the needs of your car, but this is a good starter kit. Keep in mind that belt buckles really do a number on your car's paint, so add some kind of fender cover to the repair kit as well. Even if you don't invest in a professional rubber-backed cover at least be sure to use a blanket when you lean over the fender to work under the hood. The truly committed consumer will also purchase a creeper, which is a padded board on wheels designed to make you more comfortable when you work under the car. (If you don't own a creeper use a piece of foam rubber or even the pad from your lawn furniture. You won't be able to roll around like you would on a creeper, but it's more comfortable than lying on concrete.)

Once you have the tools and the time, grab your Car Care Binder and owner's manual and get set to scout.

Scouting Trip Checklist

INTERIOR CHECK

Lights

✔ Check brake lights, turn signals, and all interior lights, such as the glovebox light, overhead light, trunk light, etc. If a bulb requires replacing, add it to your list of Small Repairs. (See Chapter 7.)

Horn

✔ Ensure horn works properly. If you encounter a problem with a stuck horn, or you're dissatisfied with its sound, add it to your list of Small Repairs. (See Chapter 6.)

Clean the Interior

✔ Identify stains and spills, and clean them immediately. (See Chapter 4.)

✔ Vacuum the rugs, and use an approved cleaning agent for vinyl or leather upholstery.

✔ Dust the dashboard.

✔ Polish window interiors.

EXTERIOR CHECK

Paint and Exterior Finish

✔ Look for nicks or chips that have to be filled in. (See Chapter 4, p. 77.)

✔ Use a cleaning solvent to remove bird droppings, which could eat into the finish of your car's paint, a problem only compounded by exposure to direct sunlight.

✔ Spray a little water on the hood and see if it beads up. If it doesn't, schedule a good wax job. (Don't be concerned about causing water marks on the hood because you'll conclude your scouting trip by washing the car.)

Shocks and Struts

✔ Push down on the hood as hard as you can and then step back to observe the bounce. The vehicle should bounce once and return to position; if it continues to bounce like a yo-yo, add this to your list of problems for the repair shop. (See Chapter 7, p. 168.)

✔ Observe the front of the car from a few feet away. Does it appear to sag on one side? This could indicate a suspension problem, so add it to your list for the repair shop.

Windshield Wiper Blades

✔ Check for hardness, roughness, or cracking. If the blades are pliable and smooth, just wipe the edges with a cloth and window cleaner solvent.

✔ If the blades indicate it's time for a change, add this to your list of small repairs. (See Chapter 7, p. 168.)

Doors, Hatches, and Hinges

✔ Open and close all hinged doors, hatches, and the trunk. If you detect a squeak or the door doesn't move smoothly, oil the hinges. (See Chapter 5.)

✔ While you're checking the doors and hatches, examine the weather strips around the doors' edges. Lubricate them with a silicone cleaning agent to keep them supple, because supple weather strips seal better than ones that are dry or worn.

✔ If the weather strips have suffered severe deterioration, add them to your list for the repair shop.

Tires

✔ Inspect tires closely for uneven wear or for the appearance of wear bars (see Chapter 7, p. 163) that may indicate underlying problems. Add suspicious findings to your repair shop list.

✔ Check the depth of the tread. In states requiring safety inspections, tread requirements are at least 1/16 inch. (For

Close view, tire with tread

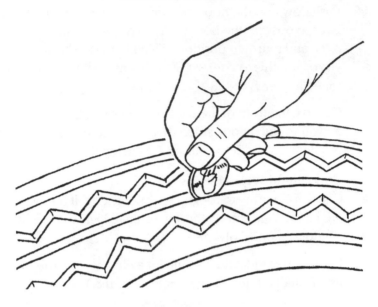

The distance between Lincoln's head and
top of tread indicates tire wear.

some reason I can't begin to fathom, manuals often refer to
this measurement as 2/32 inch instead of the reduced frac-
tion of 1/16 inch. Of course, they mean the same thing, so
look for either in your owner's manual or the information
you consult.) Since 1/16 inch is nearly impossible to judge by
sight, you can check the tread using a Lincoln-head penny.
Insert the penny, Lincoln-head first, into the most worn part
of the tire. If you can see the top of Lincoln's head the tire
will not pass inspection, but if some of the head is buried in
the groove, the tire has enough tread to be considered safe.

✔ Check air pressure with a tire gauge, making sure you insert
it in the tire valve at a perfectly straight angle so you don't
let air escape. Check not only the tires on your car but also
your spare tire or donut spare in the trunk. Air pressure
specifications for tires are listed in your owner's manual. If a

tire is low, add it to your list of small repairs. You can fill the tire at a service station at the end of your scouting trip.

✔ Check the maintenance records in your Car Care Binder to see if it's time to rotate the tires. I recommend 5,000 miles as a good change interval. (See Chapter 5.)

Trunk Inspection

✔ Move to the rear of your car and open the trunk. Check the inside for moisture or rust, indicating a water leak.

✔ Vacuum the interior and clean any plastic or metal parts. Did you know used car appraisers pay particular attention to the trunk's condition when evaluating a car? For this reason alone, it pays to keep your trunk nice and clean.

Undercarriage Inspection

✔ Jack up the car to check the condition of the undercarriage. If you don't have the floor jack and jack stands required to jack up your car safely, get on your hands and knees and use a flashlight for a better look.

✔ Check for signs of salt or mud buildup. When you wash your car at the end of your scouting trip, pay close attention to these areas.

✔ Check parts on the undercarriage and the ground for leaks. (See Chapter 7, p. 180.)

✔ If you have equipment to jack up the car safely, grab a flashlight and lie down on your creeper. Once you've got a good view of the undercarriage, examine the exhaust system for rust, wear, or loose parts. If you have a front-wheel-drive car, also check the axle boots for tears or breaks. (See Chapter 7, p. 168.)

✔ If you have any questions or doubts about the undercarriage, put them on your list for the repair shop. Once the car is in the hands of the auto technician, ask if you can observe while the car is up on a lift.

Under the Hood

Battery Terminals

✔ Check for corrosion or loose connections. Tighten connections and clean as necessary. (See Chapter 4.)

✔ If your battery is not maintenance-free, check to see if it's time to add water. (See Chapter 5.)

✔ With a rag and a baking soda/water solution, clean the top and sides of the battery. A dirty battery can drain a few amps of electricity, and while it may not seem like much, every little bit counts.

Air Cleaner

✔ Remove the lid and check the air filter for dirt. (See Chapter 5.) You can vacuum a paper air filter if the dust is dry and not sticky with an accumulation of oil. Clean a foam filter with dishwashing detergent and water—although it's such an inexpensive part, I prefer to just replace it rather than go to the bother of cleaning it.

✔ If the filter is very dirty, either add an air filter to your shopping list for the auto parts store or add this to your list of Small Repairs or your Stuff for the Repair Shop list.

Engine Assessment

✔ Is the engine covered with a film of grease? An engine covered with grease and road dirt runs hotter, so clean it by spraying the area with a detergent such as Spic-N-Span mixed with water and then towel it dry—*if* your car is a pre-1980 model.

A clean engine area means you respect and appreciate your car, and any technician who opens the hood and sees a clean engine will respect and appreciate you. But *never* hose down the engine area on a later-model car. They just have too many electrical components that can be damaged. Repair shops used to recommend steam cleaning, but, once again, with today's sophisticated electronic equipment even that's too risky.

If You Perform Only One Task Mentioned in This Book...

I know a lot of people out there are fascinated by the how-to movement. (Who among us hasn't watched a cooking show on television even though we had absolutely no intention of trying the recipe?) I call this to your attention because some of you may be fascinated by the *idea* of car care and enjoying this book immensely, but despite your best intentions, you don't think you'll ever really get around to following every last point I present. Well, highlight the one about engine oil, because *it's the single most important bit of maintenance you can do on your car.* I can't begin to stress strongly enough how quickly neglect in this area ruins an engine. If you perform just one assignment that you learn from this book, make it faithful attention to the engine oil!

Engine Oil

✔ Check the engine oil level and add more if indicated. If it's time for an oil change (most auto technicians recommend every three months or 3,000 miles as the appropriate change interval), either do it yourself or add it to your list for the repair shop. (See Chapter 5.)

Radiator

✔ Clean debris and insect carcasses from the exterior of the radiator. (See Chapter 5.)

Radiator Hoses and Heater Hoses

✔ Radiator and heater hoses are prone to split if they're dry and hard, so inspect them for a brittle condition or any small cracks. Pay particular attention to where the clamps tighten on the hoses. A crack means something will leak. You may be able to identify the crack by looking for patches of dried coolant, which look kind of whitish, like dried salt marks.

✔ Really squishy hoses can collapse just like a baby bottle nipple being sucked shut. Feel the hoses; if any feel extremely soft and easy to squeeze, put them on your Stuff for the Repair Shop list for replacing. (See Chapter 7, p. 166.)

Belts
✔ Look for dryness or cracks on the inside part of the belt that rides on the pulley. If the cracks are deep, replace them soon. (See Chapter 4.)

✔ Newer belts have a time schedule for replacement; check your owner's manual for its recommendation.

Coolant
✔ Check the level of coolant in the overflow reservoir. You're okay if it's more than half full. If not, add more coolant. (See Chapter 5.)

✔ If the coolant is murky or rusty, it's time to flush the cooling system. Add that to your list of Small Repairs. (See Chapter 4.)

Windshield Washer Reservoir
✔ Fill the reservoir to the proper level every time you do a scouting trip. (See Chapter 5.)

Power Steering Reservoir
✔ Remove the cap (it will be marked in most models) and check the level using the little dipstick attached to the cap. Add more if necessary. (See Chapter 4.)

✔ If you detect signs of a leak, add it to your list of things to be checked at the repair shop.

Transmission Fluid

✔ Judge the condition of transmission fluid by checking its color. (See Chapter 5.)

✔ Check the level of transmission fluid. Since there's a tendency to get "splash readings," repeat the process several times until the results are consistent. Add fluid as indicated by your reading. (See Chapter 5.)

✔ The need to add fluid suggests a leak, so search for its source. (See Chapter 7, p. 183.) Note your findings on the Stuff for the Repair Shop list.

Road Test Check

✔ Time for a test drive. You mean business on this trip so turn off the radio and pay attention to the ride. This way you can hear any unusual sounds and give the vehicle's performance your full attention.

✔ Evaluate the car on a variety of road conditions, including in-the-city driving, open highways, and hills.

✔ Pay close attention to how well the car brakes.

✔ Record in your Car Care Binder any difference in the car's performance during varying weather conditions.

✔ See Chapter 7 for a detailed list of criteria to evaluate performance during the road test.

Congratulations! You've nearly completed the scouting trip. Review your list to confirm small repairs you'll handle yourself, those best left to the repair shop, and items for routine maintenance. Now perform a little triage by determining which repairs will be handled when, make an appointment at the repair shop, and, most important, stick to the schedule.

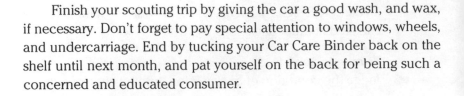

Finish your scouting trip by giving the car a good wash, and wax, if necessary. Don't forget to pay special attention to windows, wheels, and undercarriage. End by tucking your Car Care Binder back on the shelf until next month, and pat yourself on the back for being such a concerned and educated consumer.

4

Advice from a Road Scholar:

Quick Fix-It

Answers for the

Maintenance-Impaired

Y ou've finished your scouting trip, so now it's time to roll up your sleeves and tackle items on your first list, Small Repairs—but you've got to be realistic. Again and again I've told you about the sophistication of today's cars, which means there are fewer and fewer repairs a car owner should, or even *could,* attempt. Before you start brandishing a wrench, let's go over some ground rules.

The Rules of Repair

✔ As a consumer, you do more for your car by maintaining it properly than by attempting tough repairs. If you're really dying to get your hands dirty, rest assured proper car maintenance offers a long list of fascinating possibilities.

✔ If you are determined to cultivate the skills of a serious auto technician, visit your car dealership and order the factory service manual designed specifically for your car's make and model. This manual gives step-by-step instructions for a variety of procedures and is worth the $40 to $50 investment. Keep in mind, however, it was designed for professionals, so you might find the information difficult to digest. If so, check your local bookstore for a less expensive version geared toward amateurs.

✔ Enlist the help of an experienced technician—or at least a do-it-yourselfer with a confirmed track record—to advise you the first time you attempt a repair. If you don't happen to have an expert handy, ask at the auto parts store. The employees may be able to suggest someone, but it's also not unheard-of for a salesperson to join you in the parking lot to take a peek under the hood. It's valuable advice, so take it if they offer.

✔ Some people stay away from car repairs because they're afraid they'll be injured, but your car is as safe as your house if you know the danger zones:

Electrical shock: If the hood is open but the engine isn't running, it's impossible to get an electric shock. When the engine *is* running, you are exposed to electrical current, particularly from the fatter spark plug wires carrying electrical current from the distributor.

Burns: If the engine is running or if you've recently stopped the car, you could be burned by touching the engine itself or the radiator. You also could sustain a chemical burn if you come in contact with acid from a leaking battery.

Cuts: Anytime you tinker under the hood you could cut yourself on rough edges or parts. If the engine is running, be very careful not to get a serious cut from the moving fan at the front of the engine.

Toxins: Exhaust fumes can be harmful if you work in a

closed area with the car engine running. Certain solvents and additives issue noxious fumes, and none of them should ever be inhaled or ingested. One particularly dangerous fluid is antifreeze, which looks like lime soda and even has a slightly sweet taste, but just a small amount can kill a child or a pet.

✔ The most important rule: If you are even the slightest bit uncertain about a problem or repair, back off! A well-intentioned-but-unskilled amateur often inflicts the kind of damage that falls into the categories Disastrous or Expensive (often both). I know because I've seen plenty of them towed into my shop.

The Small Repairs

Now that you understand the ground rules, let's get started. Your confidence will build each time you master a new repair, and by the time you finish the projects here and in the section on routine maintenance, I guarantee you'll be hooked on car care for life.

Cleaning Battery Terminals

Corrosion around the battery terminals affects the way electrical currents are conducted, and if the corrosion is severe it can even prevent the car from starting. Sometimes you'll be able to see a kind of whitish powder develop on the terminals, but most problems are caused by corrosion you *can't* see at the contact surfaces between the terminal and the post.

You will need:

A 1/2-inch or 5/6-inch box wrench or an open-end wrench from your tool kit or a small ratchet wrench designed specifically for side terminals. Use a 10M (metric measurements) wrench for imports.

screwdriver or battery cable terminal puller

battery terminal cleaner brush

rag

water and baking soda solution

petroleum jelly

NOTE: *Never* smoke cigarettes or use anything that might spark around a battery. To avoid electrical shock, perform the following procedure in the following sequence:

1. Use the wrench to loosen the nuts on the battery terminals at the end of the cable. Be sure to note which is the negative terminal and which is the positive terminal. They will be clearly marked, and the positive cable is almost always red.

2. Use the battery cable terminal puller to remove the negative terminal. If you do not own this tool, use your fingers to work the cable back and forth until it is loosened, or insert a screwdriver underneath the terminal and gently pry it up.

3. Use the battery terminal cleaner brush to scrub the inside of the hole in the terminal. Brush until the surface is shiny like new metal. Then fit the other side of the tool over the battery post and rotate it until the metal shines.

4. Dip a rag in the water/baking soda solution and clean the top of the battery, removing metal particles that were brushed off the terminal and posts.

5. Repeat Step 2 through 4 with the positive terminal.

6. Return the terminals to the proper posts, positive *first,* then negative. Tighten the bolts until you cannot turn the terminal any more.

7. Apply a light coating of petroleum jelly to the outside of the terminals to fight future corrosion buildup.

Battery Replacement

There may come a time when your car needs a new battery but it isn't cooperative enough to go dead near a repair shop. If you want to avoid the cost of towing, you can replace the battery on your own.

You will need:

water

baking soda

rag or brush

1. Disconnect the battery terminals. (See "Cleaning Battery Terminals" on p. 55.)

2. Loosen the bolt on the clamp holding the battery in place. It may be located at either the top or the bottom of the battery, so look carefully because the hold-down bracket is clearly visible.

3. Lift the battery out of the car and use a rag dipped in a water/baking soda solution to clean its top. If corrosion is thick, use a brush to clean it.

4. Clean the tray on which the battery sits with the water/baking soda solution.

5. Take your old battery to a reputable parts store or repair shop and ask them to test it. Many people just assume a battery is shot, but another problem could be causing your battery to discharge.

6. Recharge the battery if it's good. If it's bad, buy a quality new one. Junk batteries have some value so inquire if the store will take your old battery and count it as credit toward the purchase of a new one.

7. Set your new or recharged battery on the battery tray and tighten the clamp to hold it in place.

8. Clean the battery cables and reattach them. (See "Cleaning Battery Terminals" on p. 55.)

Battery in tray

battery

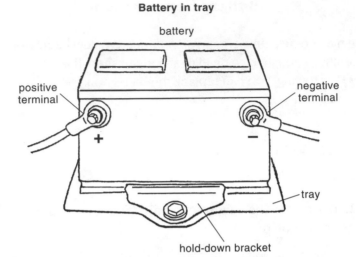

positive
terminal

negative
terminal

+

−

tray

hold-down bracket

Replacing Spark Plugs and Spark Plug Wires

The lifetime of a spark plug varies depending on the condition of the engine, type of ignition and fuel system, and the kind of driving you do. Consult your owner's manual for the factory recommendation.

You can change spark plugs and spark plug wires (technically called *ignition cables*) or just the spark plugs alone, but if you've already driven more than 30,000 miles and you're changing the plugs, check the wires too. Most wires last for over 50,000 miles, so you won't have to replace them every time you replace the plugs. If your maintenance schedule indicates it's time to change both the spark plugs and the wires, you'll find a variety to choose from at the parts store. In my opinion it's best to stick with original equipment plugs (e.g., AC Delco for General Motors cars, Motorcraft for Ford, etc.). Ask at the parts store if you're unsure of the original equipment for your vehicle. I know mechanics who suggest using a "hotter" or "cooler" plug, but call me old-fashioned because I like to stick with factory specifications, and I advise that you do too.

Before you start this repair, lift the hood and make sure you can locate every spark plug before you remove any parts. This used to be a repair anyone could try, but some later-model cars now place spark plugs in tight locations. Unless you have access to every one of your car's spark plugs, leave this repair for the professionals.

You will need:

spark plug socket (with insulation inside) ratchet handle
rag
feeler gauge to gap spark plugs
replacement spark plugs
1 set of spark plug wires

1. Consult your owner's manual (or ask at the parts store) for the spark plug specifications for your car and engine.

2. To avoid error, replace only one plug and wire at a time. Spark plugs fire in a particular sequence and it varies from car to car. If you mix up the plugs and wires, you'll screw up the firing sequence, and then you've bought yourself all kinds of problems so intimidating that you'll never try to fix anything again.

3. By hand, gently twist and pull the plug wire off the first spark plug. (If you are not replacing the plug wires at this time, take special care not to damage them.) Remove the other end of the wire from the distributor cap.

4. Use a rag to wipe clean any loose dirt or grease around the spark plug.

5. Refer to the back of the ratchet handle, which has a little arm with two positions, one clockwise and one counterclockwise. Plugs loosen counterclockwise and tighten clockwise. Since you'll be removing plugs, set the ratchet for counterclockwise by setting the arm to "on" for clockwise and "off" for counterclockwise.

6. Gently but firmly place the spark plug socket over the plug, then insert the square end of the ratchet handle into the top of the socket. By ratching the handle, the socket will turn counterclockwise and remove the spark plug.

7. Use the feeler gauge to gap the new spark plug according to the specifications. "Gapping" means you're adjusting the

Replacing spark plugs

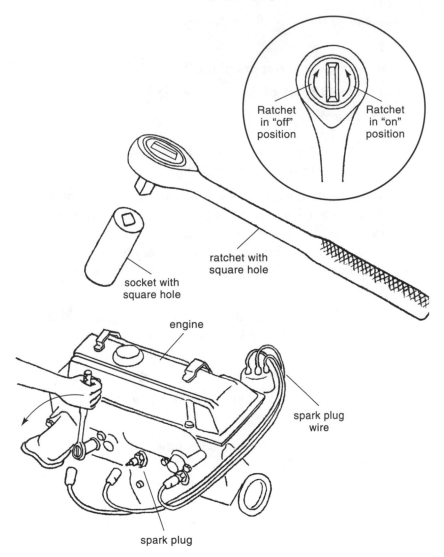

Ratchet in "off" position

Ratchet in "on" position

ratchet with square hole

socket with square hole

engine

spark plug wire

spark plug

space on the hooklike electrode of the spark plug's firing side. There are various readings along the edge of the feeler gauge. Select the one for your engine's specifications. Be sure to check your owner's manual because specs vary from .020 to .060.

8. If you are replacing spark plug wires, take the wire you just removed and compare it to the new wires. Select a new wire that matches the length of the old one.

9. Install the newly gapped spark plug by hand, turning until it is finger-tight. Next, adjust the arm on the ratchet handle to the "clockwise" position and use it to tighten the plug further. (Using the ratchet before finger-tightening could result in damaged threads in the engine block, and that's a serious mistake.)

10. Attach one end of the spark plug wire to the plug, pressing firmly until it is seated and the rubber boot (cover) is on properly. Attach the other end of the wire to the distributor cap in the same manner.

11. Repeat this procedure until all of the spark plugs and/or wires have been replaced.

Radiator Cap Removal

The radiator and radiator cap play important roles in many small repairs, but removal of the cap can be hazardous unless it's done correctly. If the car has not been running and the engine is cold, the radiator cap is safe to be removed immediately. However, if the car has been running, even a short distance, *do not* attempt to remove the cap. Radiator caps pressurize the cooling system, raising the boiling point of the coolant proportionally so the system can run hotter without boiling over. Removing the radiator cap when the engine and radiator are hot allows steam and scalding liquid to shoot out.

1. If your engine overheats, turn it off and give it at least twenty minutes to cool down. Park the car in the shade if possible and open the hood. Never attempt to add cold water to a hot engine, because it could crack the engine block. (For additional instructions about overheated engines, see Chapter 6.)

2. After the system is sufficiently cooled, place a rag or a thick towel over the radiator cap, press down hard, and turn the cap counterclockwise to the first notch. After initial pressure escapes, continue turning cap counterclockwise until you can remove it. Some radiators have a safety cap equipped with a little lever to allow pressure to exhaust. If your car has this feature, cover the safety cap with a rag and open it, then remove the cap.

3. When replacing the radiator cap, be sure to turn it to the lock position.

Flushing the Cooling System

It's time to flush the cooling system when coolant appears murky or rusty (something you'd check during your monthly scouting trip, and prior to winter and summer). There are two ways to flush your cooling system; I suggest you refer to your owner's manual to see if the manufacturer prefers one over the other, or discuss it with your favorite technician.

Method #1: Prepared Kit

Auto parts stores sell inexpensive flushing kits. The benefit to using one of these prepared kits is that it flushes the entire system, not just the radiator. Kits come complete with a tee fitted for a hose connection, and all you have to do is follow the directions.

You will need:

flushing kit (purchased at auto parts store)

garden hose and water

antifreeze

1. Kit instructions will point you to one of your car's hoses, which you will cut and, using hose clamps, attach the tee.

Flushing the Cooling System: Neatness Counts

The flushed water will run down the sides of the radiator and make a mess under the car, so do this procedure parked on concrete. You don't want to find yourself
stuck in the mud once you've finished. You may want to
place a bucket under your car to catch the fluid, but this
repair is rather messy and the antifreeze is likely to
splash.

Once you're through flushing the cooling system, be
sure to clean up any antifreeze spills thoroughly. Remember, antifreeze is highly toxic, and you don't want any of
the neighborhood dogs lapping it up.

2. Connect your garden hose to the top of the tee.

3. Remove the radiator cap (see instructions on p. 61,
   "Radiator Cap Removal") and then turn on the water
   spigot connected to the garden hose. Water will travel
   through the system, entering at the tee and coming out the
   opening of the radiator. Continue to run water until it
   comes out clear.

4. Turn off the water and add the proper amount of antifreeze
   through the top of the radiator. (See Chapter 6.) Water re-
   maining in the system at this time will be forced out of the
   tee.

5. Put the cap (it comes with the kit) on the tee and replace the
   radiator cap.

Method #2

You will need:

container to catch antifreeze, such as an old dishpan

garden hose and water

antifreeze

coolant level tester

1. Position the container under the radiator tank.

2. Locate the *petcock,* a small faucet with a handle that you'll find on the lower tank of the radiator, inside facing the rear of the car. Turn the handle of the petcock to the open position, and coolant will immediately begin to drain into the container under the car.

3. Properly dispose of antifreeze. (See antifreeze packaging for instructions.)

4. After the coolant has drained completely, remove the radiator cap (see instructions on p. 61, "Radiator Cap Removal") and insert the nozzle of the garden hose. Turn on the water and let it run until it passes through the system and drains clear.

5. Turn the petcock handle back to the closed position.

6. Consult your owner's manual (or ask at the auto parts store) to determine how much coolant your car's cooling system will hold. *(note: The coolant mixture is 50 percent antifreeze and 50 percent water.)* First add the proper amount of antifreeze to the radiator, then add the water.

7. Run the engine for a few minutes, *never* in a closed garage and not long enough to get it hot. Then recheck the coolant level. It should be up to the neck of the radiator, so add more water if necessary. (See Chapter 5, p. 63 for tester instructions.)

Engine side of a Radiator

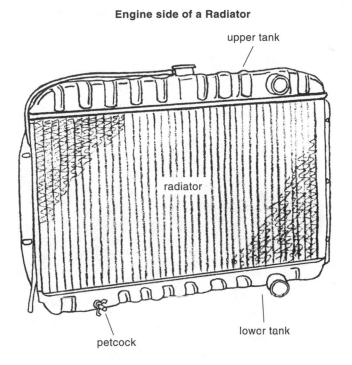

Adding Power Steering Fluid

Locate the power steering reservoir. If you're having trouble finding it, look for the crankshaft pulley since a belt drives the power steering pump.

You will need:

rag

new power steering fluid or automatic transmission fluid (consult your owner's manual)

1. Turn the lid, which sits on top of a three-inch-high throat, counterclockwise to remove it. The dipstick is connected to the lid.

2. Wipe off the dipstick, insert it, and then remove it again. Read the level marked on the dipstick.

Location of the power steering reservoir

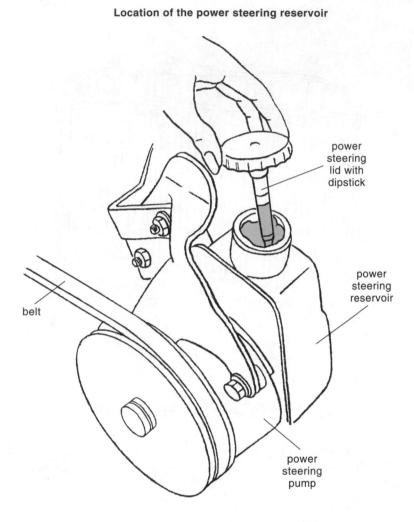

power
steering
lid with
dipstick

power
steering
reservoir

belt

power
steering
pump

3. If you have to add fluid, check your owner's manual for type and instructions. Some cars require a special power steering fluid, but others call for automatic transmission fluid.

4. Remember to check for the source of any leaks.

Replacing Radiator Hoses

You'll detect bad radiator hoses during your monthly scouting trip, and as a smart car consumer, you will replace a hose immediately because it's much easier than dealing with an overheated engine.

Take a good look at the suspicious hose to ensure you can reach the clamps at each end. If you can't, let the repair shop handle the repair. If this is something you think you can tackle, make sure you purchase the correct replacement hose. Radiator hoses are preformed, and you must have the one your car requires. If you can, take the old hose to the auto parts store so you can compare it; otherwise, you're at the mercy of the store. The salesperson will need the car's year, model, and engine size to determine the right configuration.

You will need:

pair of heavy pliers

large, standard screwdriver

replacement hose

replacement clamps (purchase the gear-type that tighten easily by turning a screw)

bucket or large container (especially if you're replacing a lower hose)

steel wool or a rag

antifreeze

1. Look at the clamps to determine which kind you have. They will be either wire-type clamps (constructed out of heavy wire) or screw-type clamps (circles of metal held together at the end with screws). Factories install wire clamps because they are cheaper, but when it comes time to replace them you'll use the higher-quality screw-type clamp. (The screw clamps are standard for replacements. You wouldn't even be able to find the wire clamps in an auto parts store.) Use pliers to remove the old clamps and discard them.

Clamps and hose connections

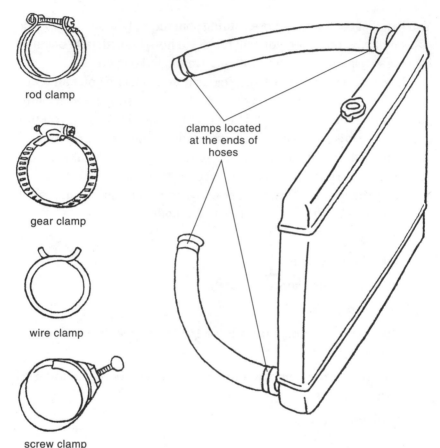

rod clamp

gear clamp

wire clamp

screw clamp

clamps located
at the ends of
hoses

2. Remove the hose. You may find it difficult to pull the hose off the outlet pipe. Twist the hose first and, if necessary, gently pry with a screwdriver, but be very careful not to puncture the pipe. Coolant will drain into the bucket.

3. Clean the pipe ends with steel wool or a rag.

4. Starting with the end that is less accessible, slip the new clamp over the end of the hose, then slip the hose over the pipe. Being careful not to overtighten, secure the clamp on the hose. Repeat the procedure at the other side of the hose and pipe.

5. If the coolant you caught in the bucket is clean, clear, and green, remove the radiator cap and reuse it. If the coolant appears murky or rusty, replace with fresh antifreeze and water (using a 50-50 mixture). If it's really nasty-looking, flush the cooling system at this time. (See Chapter 4, p. 62.)

One final word about replacing hoses: If you find signs that one hose has to be replaced, it's best to replace them all. After all, they're the same age and they've faced the same operating conditions, so if one goes, others will soon follow.

Sealing Cooling System Leaks

Auto parts stores offer a number of products, commonly given the generic name Stop-Leak, designed to seal leaks in the cooling system. Ask your auto technician if this product is right for the problem with your car. Typically Stop-Leak is effective if there's a very slight leak losing only a few drops at a time and if you don't have to add water frequently. If the leak is severe, however, take the car to the shop for repairs because the problem is beyond Stop-Leak's capabilities.

You will need:

can of Stop-Leak (Get a brand recommendation from your auto technician.)

1. Read all product directions carefully before using.

2. Remove the radiator cap and pour the product into the top of the radiator. As it circulates with the coolant, the Stop-Leak will fill small openings. (See Chapter 4, p. 61 "Radiator Cap Removal")

3. If the leak continues, consult your auto technician. *Never* add more Stop-Leak if the first application didn't work; too much can clog the cooling system.

Additive Alert

I constantly notice advertising for additives for the car. You'll find additives for the engine, transmission, power steering, cooling system. In short, if there's an opening there's an additive, and they all claim to do anything from performance enhancement to complete repair. It's like buying a miracle in a can, if you believe the commercials.

The thing is, I *don't* believe in miracles.

My advice to you is to perform all the proper maintenance on your car and do it consistently, following the manufacturer's recommendations. Ignore the additives unless your auto technician suggests one specific product as a solution to a particular problem. Additives for your car are kind of like tonics for your body. A person could go broke buying all of the miracle products that claim to make you look better/feel better/stay young forever, but if your physician told you to buy one specific remedy for one specific health problem, it might be worth a try.

I'm not just trying to warn you against wasting money here. Many additives are not only unnecessary and expensive, some actually can be harmful to your car.

Here's a scenario: You have a leak that appears to be transmission fluid. Instead of taking the car to the repair shop, you head to your auto parts store and invest $10 or $15 in some powerful Stop-Leak additive, which you promptly pour into the transmission. The product claims to act chemically on the neoprene seals to make them swell, thus stopping the leak, and you rock proudly on your heels thinking you've just solved the problem.

But . . .

The leak continues. So you pour in some more of the Stop-Leak additive. The next thing you know, the transmission starts doing some weird things—weird enough to suggest a trip to the repair shop. There you listen to the auto technician explain that the transmission needs a complete overhaul. To the soundtrack of cash registers ringing, the technician tells you how the Stop-Leak additive acted on some internal operational seals and that the initial leak was really from a simple pan gasket, which would have cost you less than $40 to fix.

The moral of the story is to check with your auto technician before you pour anything into your car. And unless the tech tells you otherwise, leave those additives on the auto store shelf.

Serpentine Belts

Many new cars feature a serpentine belt that winds around and operates everything. Cars equipped with such belts have a diagram under the hood that gives you a kind of road map detailing the belt's path, but it's tricky. Attempt to replace a serpentine belt only if you have an experienced friend nearby.

Replacing the Fan Belt

On older cars, one single fan belt drove the alternator, fan, and the water pump. Depending on the number of accessories, however, most cars on the road today use multiple belts. If you have to disengage other belts to get to a worn fan belt, I suggest you take the car to the shop for repair. But if the multiple-belt removal looks extremely simple, or if it's a single-belt system, you can address the problem personally.

You will need:

replacement fan belt

wooden hammer

large, standard screwdriver

belt tension gauge (optional)

1. To remove the fan belt, first you'll have to locate the *alternator pivot bolt*. It's mounted to the lower bracket holding the alternator. The *adjustment nut* is on the alternator bracket with the long slot. Loosen the pivot bolt and the adjustment nut with an open-end or box wrench, and finally push the alternator in until there's enough slack to allow you to remove the fan belt.

**Alternator pivot bolt and alternator adjustment nut,
in relation to the fan belt**

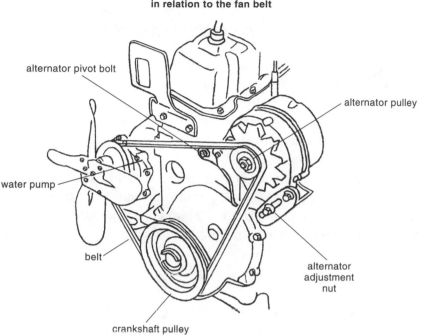

alternator pivot bolt

alternator pulley

water pump

belt

alternator adjustment nut

crankshaft pulley

2. Remove the fan belt from the crankshaft pulley and from the alternator pulley.

3. Put the new belt over the crankshaft, water pump, and alternator pulleys. It should fit flush into the grooves of the pulley. If the fan belt is tight going on, even with the alternator pushed in, or if it's loose once it's in place, you may have the wrong size belt. Compare the new one to the old belt or ask at the auto parts store to make sure you have the correct replacement belt.

4. Return the alternator to its original position until the belt fits snugly. Using the handle of a wooden hammer (or your thumb, if you're particularly strong), push in on the belt until you have about 1/2 inch of play. The proper tension on a belt is extremely important: If it's loose, it will slip on the pulleys,

When to Replace Fan Belts

Fan belts in older cars give clues to impending failure. Their rubber-coated fabric cover frays as the belts wear down. Since material used in the design of new fan belts doesn't give as many clues to wear and tear, manufacturers recommend replacing belts on later-model cars every four years.

I'll pass along one final tip about fan belts: When you replace a belt, leave the old one in your trunk in case of an emergency. Even a used belt looks pretty good when you're broken down in the middle of nowhere!

and if it's too tight, it will damage the components it drives. Without experience it's difficult to judge the play in the belt, so if you're new at this repair, purchase an inexpensive tool called a belt tension gauge. Simple instructions come with the gauge that direct you to the proper connection to the belt and specifications for the adjustment.

5. After adjusting the tension, tighten the alternator's adjustment bolt and pivot bolt.

6. Once you've driven the car for 100 miles or so, check the tension of the fan belt again and adjust as necessary.

Replacing the Thermostat

If your themostat sticks open, your heater won't provide warmth until you've driven a pretty fair distance. If it sticks closed, your car overheats. Either way you'll want to fix the problem, but first be sure that the thermostat is the cause of the overheating.

You can remove the thermostat and test it very easily. The valve

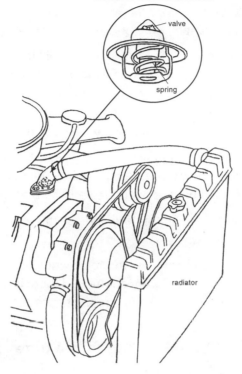

Thermostat in relation to radiator

valve

spring

radiator

should be closed when it's cold so nothing flows through. (The thermostat is clearly faulty if it's open while you're holding it in your hand.) Next boil a pan of water, tie a string to the thermostat, and lower it into the water. If the valve opens when it is exposed to this heat, it's okay. If it remains closed in the boiling water, then you know it's bad and you should replace it. You will need:

bucket to catch coolant

replacement thermostat

screwdriver

wrench

1. Locate the thermostat. It is almost always located where the top radiator hose connects to the engine.

2. Place the bucket under the radiator hose to catch the coolant.

3. Use a screwdriver to loosen the clamp holding the radiator hose so you can move the hose out of the way, being careful to drain coolant into the bucket.

4. Using the proper wrench from your tool kit (size will vary depending on your car), remove the bolts holding the thermostat housing in place. Remove the thermostat and look carefully for its old gasket because it may come off in pieces and you certainly don't want it floating around in the cooling system.

5. Put the new gasket in place, making sure the holes line up, then put the new thermostat in spring-side down. Replace the housing, then use the wrench to put the bolts back in.

6. Reconnect the radiator hose and use the screwdriver to tighten the clamp.

7. Remove the radiator cap and return the coolant to the radiator. (Since coolant has been drained there is no danger from compressed steam, so you can safely unscrew the cap.)

Replacing the PCV Valve

The positive crankcase ventilation valve, or PCV valve, plays the most important role in your emissions system, recycling unused gases that get through the combustion process. A malfunctioning PCV valve will exhibit several symptoms, including a rough idle or poor gas mileage. Faulty PVC valves also can cause pressure to build up, resulting in engine oil leaks, so check for this problem if your car has excessive oil leaks. Manufacturers usually recommend a once-a-year replacement for this part, so refer to your owner's manual.

This valve is usually located at the end of a hose connected to a valve cover. To test the PCV valve, pull it out from its rubber grommet in the valve cover and shake it. If you hear a rattle, it's probably okay.

You can also check the PCV valve with the engine running. While it's still connected to the hose—but out of the valve cover—put your finger on the end of the PCV valve. If it's working you'll feel suction and hear a click that proves the valve is moving. If not, you can proceed to replace the PCV valve.

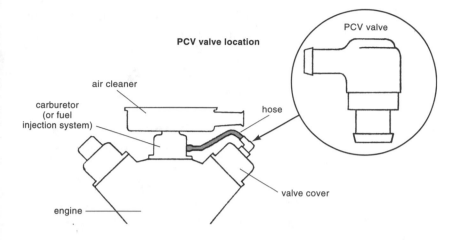

PCV valve location

PCV valve

air cleaner

carburetor
(or fuel
injection system)

hose

valve cover

engine

You will need:

screwdriver

replacement PCV valve

1. Loosen the hose clamp with a screwdriver and slide it up on the hose.

2. By hand, pull the PCV valve out of the hose and insert the new one in its place.

3. Position the hose clamp and tighten it.

4. Push the PCV valve back into its grommet in the valve cover.

Repairing Chips and Nicks in Paint

Paint on later-model cars is rust-resistant, but on early-model cars small nicks and chips can turn into big patches of rust, so the next time someone dings your car door in the parking lot, take a few minutes to touch it up. Auto parts stores offer a selection of replacement paints and touch-up kits, so select one that matches your car's finish and follow the kit's instructions. (They vary by product.)

A couple of tips about do-it-yourself paint touch ups: Kits often come with a brush, but you'll have more control and less smudging if you toss the brush and use the torn end of a match out of a matchbook instead.

Also, clear nail polish is a good substitute if you care about stopping the rust but don't want to bother with the cosmetics of matching paint.

Cleaning Upholstery

Don't leave a stain to set in your upholstery. Worse than looking unattractive, some of them start to smell after a while. (Spilled milk is the worst offender.) If your car has a leather or vinyl interior, use an approved cleaner from the auto parts store. If your car's upholstery is fabric, you can choose from the variety of car upholstery cleaners, but really, any household fabric or carpet cleaner will do.

You will need:

dry towel

gentle scrub brush

laundry detergent or carpet cleaner

water

1. Dip the scrub brush into a solution of water and detergent and lightly brush away stain. Tougher stains may have to be treated with undiluted carpet cleaner.

2. Pat the area with a towel and then allow the upholstery to air-dry completely.

If you managed not only to stain your upholstery but to tear it too, I recommend you see a professional for repairs. Don't go into a panic thinking this will be an expensive repair. Often car interiors are designed with many different panels of fabric, and replacing just one square of material is cheaper than you'd think.

Now that you've got some small repairs under your belt, let's move on to items you'll encounter most frequently as you follow a schedule of routine maintenance aimed at enhancing your vehicle's performance and appearance.

5

Take Two Quarts of Oil and Call Me in the Morning: A Maintenance Schedule You Can Live With

My grandmother was a clean freak. In fact, I can well remember "Cleanliness is next to godliness" ringing in my ears when she wanted my brothers and me to wash our hands before dinner. Well, my grandmother would be pleased to know I've adopted her favorite phrase and applied it to the maintenance of an automobile. Clean cars don't just look better, they run better too.

Think about what would happen if you continued to use a blender without washing it after each use. The blades would get so gummed up they wouldn't be able to rotate properly. And any homeowner can relate to what happens when a furnace filter gets dirty: All that impacted dirt restricts air flow. These days people are so into the car as "status symbol," they forget it's really just another kind of appliance. So I always tell people not to get so carried away polishing the outside that they forget the real business going on under the hood.

Keeping Your Car Shiny as New—Inside and Out

If you really want to protect a big investment, get the most for your money, and extend the life of your car, start by following this uncompromising maintenance schedule.

Air Filter

Air filters, which prevent airborne contamination such as dust and sand from entering the air/fuel mixture, are a good place for the novice to start because they're easy to locate and you can rely on your own common sense to make maintenance decisions. Failure to change air filters when needed results in poor gas mileage, and if you allow the filter to become totally blocked, the engine can't run at all. Always check your air filter during your scouting trip.

To get a good look at your air filter, simply remove the wing nut (or nuts) on the lid of the air cleaner on top of the engine. Filters are usually accordion-folded paper, but some are foam-type material; either way, you can tell if it's dirty simply by looking at it. (Remember your furnace filter!)

How often you change the filter depends on what kind of driving you do. If you drive miles every day at a dusty construction site or if you regularly pass a windy and sandy beach, you're going to have to change that air filter pretty frequently. Check your owner's manual for the manufacturer's recommendation, but also take into consideration the kind of driving you do and use common sense if it tells you to check the filter more frequently.

Engine Oil and Oil Filter

You're probably more familiar with checking and changing engine oil than any other kind of maintenance. Even if you've never done it your-

Air filter and its location

wing nut

air cleaner cover

air filter

fuel system carburetor
(same parts with fuel
system fuel-injection)

air cleaner assembly

self, you still know that it has to be checked and changed at regular intervals, and, I hope, you keep up on it. But like so many maintenance
requirements with cars, people might know it has to be done without
having the slightest clue *why.*

An engine has a lot of moving parts, and each one has to be thoroughly lubricated to prevent wear and tear. As long as the engine is
running, an oil pump in the lower part of the engine sends oil through
passages to operate the valves and up to the top, where it lubricates

the rocker arms. After it lubricates up there, it drains back to the sump (or crankcase), where the oil pump again sucks it up and recirculates it.

With all that recirculation, you might think the oil has to be changed because it gets "worn out," but that's not the case. The real reason you have to change the oil is because it becomes contaminated by lots of different elements, including:

✔ Carbon from the combustion

✔ Moisture and acid from incomplete combustion

✔ Gums or resin from the gasoline

✔ Dust or airborne dirt that escape from the air filter

✔ Any fine metallic particles that result from engine wear

Separately these elements might not cause problems, but stick them together and they form engine oil sludge (kind of like cholesterol in your arteries) that robs the engine of its long life.

You cannot tell just by looking at engine oil if it needs to be changed. New engine oil is sort of amber in color, but due to its detergent qualities it turns black very quickly—within a few hundred miles. Just like air filters, how frequently you change engine oil has a lot to do with how often and where you drive the car. Actually, this all makes me think of the clichéd car salesperson line, "This car belonged to a little old lady who only drove it back and forth to church on Sundays." Believe it or not, that car isn't all it's cracked up to be. Once you know how a car operates, you'd be more likely to want the car that belonged to a traveling sales rep. Don't believe me? I'll explain.

Until the engine warms up to its ideal operating temperature (between 190 and 220 degrees F), combustion will be incomplete, creating acid and moisture. Definitely bad for engine oil. In average warm weather it takes five to seven miles to warm the engine to optimum operating temperature, and if the weather is very cold it could take up to fourteen miles. If you only take your car out for short trips around town—say, back and forth to church on Sundays—the engine never warms up to maximum efficiency, which means combustion will never

An Insider's Advice about Intervals

Even though manufacturers often recommend oil changes every six months or 6,000 miles, my colleagues and I recommend it every three months or 3,000 miles.

be complete, which means the engine oil is subject to more contaminants.

Manufacturers give varying guidelines for changing engine oil: They might tell you something like "every three months or every 3,000 miles, whichever comes first." If you do most of your driving on the highway, you could double those figures (six months or 6,000 miles), but if after three months your mileage is low because you've only driven short distances, you actually may have a greater need to change the oil.

Can you change your own engine oil and filter? It's possible, but for several reasons I don't recommend it. First, you have to be underneath the car, and that's going to require some costly jacking equipment to do it safely. Second, how do you dispose of the old engine oil? It's illegal to pour it down the drain or put it in the rubbish pile, once an acceptable method. And my third reason has to do with the value of experience: Too often an amateur will damage the oil plug by tightening it when it wasn't aligned properly or ruin the seal on the oil filter. Best to leave this job to a professional.

But some of you probably really like your new role as a do-it-yourself mechanic and these warnings don't discourage you. If you do want to change the oil and filter, first check your mileage or Car Care Binder schedule to make sure it's time for a change. Always check the oil with the engine turned off so the engine oil drains to the bottom pan where it can be measured accurately.

Checking the Level of Engine Oil and Adding More

1. Open the hood and locate the engine oil dipstick.

2. Withdraw the dipstick, wipe it clean with a paper towel, and reinsert.

3. Withdraw the dipstick again and note the level of oil as measured on the dipstick. Markings on the dipstick indicate the need for more engine oil, so don't add more unless the level reads "add." If you overfill the reservoir, oil just blows out and makes a real mess.

4. If the reading does indicate a need for more engine oil, remove the cap on one of the valve covers and add one quart of oil. (See p. 86 for instructions on how to choose the right type of oil for your engine.) Check the level again and add more if necessary.

NOTE: The cap for adding engine oil isn't normally marked, but you can find it if you use common sense. It will be the only cap on the valve cover, about 2 inches in diameter, with nothing else attached to it. You'd be facing a real disaster if you poured engine oil into the wrong reservoir and had to get it out, so take the extra time to double-check.

Changing the Engine Oil

If it's time to change the engine oil, find an open work area and gather all the equipment.

You will need:

car jack and jack stands

tool to remove and replace engine oil drain plug (available at the auto parts store)

container to hold old oil

engine oil filter tool (available at the auto parts store)

new oil filter (Your auto parts store representative will supply you with the proper filter once you provide the car's

Valve covers with oil cap

year, make, and engine size. Consult your owner's manual
if you don't know these specifications.)

engine oil—refer to your owner's manual for your engine
capacity (usually four or five quarts)

owner's manual (to help you locate parts)

1. The first step is to jack up the car, following the safety instructions in your owner's manual.

2. Once the car is safely up in the air, locate the engine oil plug,
which is in the center of the engine pan. Use the proper-size
socket to remove the engine oil plug and drain the old oil into
the container. Replace the plug, hand tightening before using
the socket.

3. Use the engine oil filter tool to remove the old oil filter, and then install the new filter. Make certain your tool fits your car's filter size. Be very careful not to damage the rubber seal on the filter as you do this. (It may help to dip your finger in oil and moisten the lip first.) Starting it in crooked can damage the seal, and the end result is a leak.

4. Add the proper amount of new oil in the opening on the valve cover.

5. Properly dispose of the used oil. The new engine oil's packaging should give you directions for disposal. In a nod toward public relations, a lot of repair shops will allow you to bring waste oil to them, and they'll dispose of it properly at no cost to you.

Understanding Oil Labels

Of course, long before you ever change the oil you face the challenge of buying the right kind, and if you're unfamiliar with the labeling system it could be quite a puzzle. Even if you don't change the oil yourself, I've seen attendants at gas stations tell customers when they're a quart low and then ask them what kind of oil they want. A lot of people simply don't know, and I think some of those attendants like to see people squirm—especially if the car owner is a woman.

Well, no more, because understanding the numbers and letters on the oil is easy. Let's use as an example an oil container that says "SAE 10W–40 SF." At first glance you might think you need a secret decoder ring to figure it out, but once again, it all makes sense if you know the logical needs of the car. The first part, SAE, stands for the Society of Automotive Engineers, who came up with the numbering system.

The 10W–40 refers to the *viscosity* of the oil. Viscosity means the oil's tendency to flow. According to the SAE numbering system, the thinnest oil starts at 5 and progresses to 10, 20, 30, and so on, all the way up to 90, when it would be thick enough technically to be called grease. The 5- or 10-weight oil would pour nice and fast like Karo syrup. I'd compare the higher-numbered oil to the kind of flow you'd get from molasses.

Okay, so now you've solved at least some of the mystery. The next big question: How do I know what viscosity oil to use in my car? The reason we have different viscosities of oil is because climate affects how oil flows. In very cold weather, the oil must be thin enough to move immediately and lubricate even before the engine warms up. As the engine runs the oil warms up, and once it does it has an even thinner consistency. In warm weather the engine really gets hot and thins out the oil even more, but it still has to be thick enough to lubricate the engine well.

Notice in my example of the oil label, SAE 10W–40 SF, there are two numbers, the 10 and the 40. That's because car owners who live in an area with vastly changing climates will have different oil needs depending on the weather. History saw some changes as the oil industry tried to meet these needs. Years ago, car owners in varying climates would use very lightweight oil in the winter, say 5 or 10, so the lubrication would be immediate. Then in the spring, they would have to drain the lightweight oil and fill the engine with 40-weight oil. Then no matter how hot it got in the summer, the oil wouldn't get so thin that it couldn't provide good lubrication. Good for the car, but what a pain for the car owner!

Then came multiple viscosity oils, which have the properties of lightweight oil for cold weather and heavier-weight oil for hotter months. So in our example, the 10W means the oil has the properties of 10-weight oil in the winter and 40-weight oil in the summer. Convenient and not too hard to figure out either, wouldn't you say?

Now all that leaves us to interpret is the *SF* at the end of our example. It just refers to the service group, which is the rating of the oil and its additives approved for proper use in specified engines. The service group recommended for your car will be in your owner's manual.

The last thing you might find on an oil label is some indication of whether the oil is conventional engine oil or if it's a synthetic. Although synthetics can be made from crude oil, as conventional motor oil is, they generally start out from natural gas, and they were designed to move faster than conventional mineral oil in cold weather. You'll notice a substantial difference in price; in fact, synthetics cost about four times as much as conventional oil, but they were designed to last longer. Some companies offer a lower-priced blend of synthetic and conventional motor oil, but the technicians I know don't recommend them. If you're going to go synthetic, it's recommended to go 100 percent.

When you change engine oil certainly you'll fill it with only one kind, but between changes, when you have to add a quart now and then, it's okay to mix. Different weights and types of oil—even synthetics and conventional—are all compatible. If you can't find the brand of oil recommended for your car, or if you want to try another viscosity, add new oil without bothering to drain what's already in there.

Fuel Filters

In order to keep contamination out of the carburetor or fuel injection system, gasoline also is filtered. Thankfully in the last decade we've seen such great improvements in gasoline and the way it's handled that fuel filter problems are increasingly rare. Still, they could happen, particularly if you have a diesel engine, because diesel fuel is not nearly as clean and refined as gasoline.

In most cars you'll find the fuel filter somewhere between the fuel pump and the fuel mixing system, usually in the top of the engine area. (On later-model cars it might be underneath and out of sight; if that's the case, I don't recommend you attempt this procedure.) The fuel filter looks like a canister with hose clamps on both ends, or it may screw in, and it is actually set into the fuel line. Unfortunately, because of the way the fuel filter is designed, you won't be able to check how dirty it is the way you can with an air filter, so it's best to plan for the professionals to do it each time you have an engine tune-up or a performance check.

If the pros tell you it's time to change the fuel filter, you can do it yourself as long as you don't mind the smell of gasoline or a little grease on your hands, but these instructions are for simpler, carbureted cars. I suggest you do not attempt to replace the fuel filter if you have a fuel-injected vehicle because there will be pressure in the gas line, and when you loosen the fitting, gasoline could spray you in the face.

To change the fuel filter in your older carbureted car, gather your tools before you begin.

Fuel filters

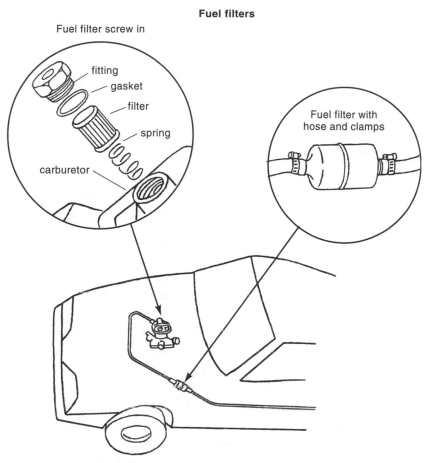

Fuel filter screw in

fitting

gasket

filter

spring

carburetor

Fuel filter with
hose and clamps

Illustrated on both carburetor and fuel-injection system

You will need:

standard screwdriver

new fuel filter

owner's manual (for locating parts)

NOTE: If the connecting hose looks dry or cracked, purchase a new one at the auto parts store. You should not reuse wire clamps, so check carefully because the new fuel filter may or may not include them in the packaging.

1. Using a screwdriver, loosen the hose clamps on each end of the filter.

2. Remove the filter with the hoses.

3. Fit the new fuel filter with hose and clamps, watching the arrow to ensure the flow is in the right direction.

Your car will send out some clues when it's time to change the fuel filter. You'll notice a bucking or sputtering when the demand for fuel is at its greatest, such as when you're driving at top speed on a highway. When you return to a slower speed, the bucking and sputtering should stop. If the clog in the fuel filter is really serious, the engine won't run at all.

Transmission Filter and Fluid

It's been my experience that many drivers know about changing the engine oil and filter, but very few are aware that they have to change the automatic transmission fluid and filter too. When it actually comes to changing the transmission filter, I'd head for the professionals because most automatic transmissions have pans on the bottom attached with twenty to thirty bolts. Since the pans don't have drain plugs as the engine oil pans do, you'll have to remove all of the bolts and gently lower the pan. Frankly, it's pretty tricky to accomplish without taking a bath in dirty transmission fluid. In fact, any time I hire an apprentice mechanic I watch him the first few times he drops a pan. When he dumps the fluid all over himself—and believe me, it's inevitable that he will—his reaction tells me a lot about his personality.

For the record, the first time I dropped a pan and took a bath in dirty transmission fluid the guys in the shop laughed so long and hard that I fled to the bathroom in tears. I was ready to quit, that's how humiliated I was, but instead I resolved to be more careful next time. You can bet I never made that mistake again (although plenty of times since I've been close enough to get a transmission fluid bath from *other mechanics'* mistakes!).

Transmission filters come in various shapes and sizes, depending on the type of transmission your car has. They're more costly than engine oil filters and the actual replacement is more labor intensive, so servicing an automatic transmission may cost you anywhere from $30 to as high as $90.

But just because I told you to have a pro change the filter doesn't mean you have no responsibility here. It's up to you to check the automatic transmission fluid so you know when it needs to be changed. I tell car owners to change the fluid on average every 24,000 miles, but we've found out time lines for any fluid changes vary, and transmission fluid is no different. The good news is you can tell just by looking at it when it's time to be changed.

You may have a difficult time finding the dipstick. The handle is marked on newer cars, but you'll have to hunt for it if you own an older model. Facing the car, the dipstick for a rear-wheel-drive automobile will be at the rear on the left side of the engine, very near the firewall. (In case you're fuzzy on what the firewall is, it's the vertical metal panel that separates the engine area from the passenger compartment. The dash is mounted to it on the inside of the car.)

In front-wheel-drive cars, the dipstick is usually located somewhere on the right side. Either refer to your owner's manual or ask an auto technician to help you locate it.

Once you locate the transmission fluid filler tube, pull out the dipstick and shake a few drops on a paper towel so you can evaluate the color. New, clean transmission fluid is bright red like cherry soda. As it oxidizes the red fades to pink, then kind of clear, followed by yellowish, then tan, and finally brown. The fluid from a transmission failure frequently turns coal black, and it's got a very nasty odor to it.

If the fluid from the dipstick test is red or pink, you're still okay. By the time it develops the yellowish tinge, it's time for a fluid change. By the way, it's wise to change at the yellow stage because really dirty transmission fluid can leave a coat of varnish on friction material parts that causes slippage and eventual failures in some older transmissions. Luckily, newer cars aren't so prone to this condition.

After you evaluate the color of the transmission fluid, it's time to check the level. The transmission dipstick offers important information needed to check your transmission fluid accurately and safely so be sure to read it before you begin.

Checking the Level of Transmission Fluid

You will need:

paper towel

funnel

new transmission fluid

1. Park the car on a level surface, warmed up and with the transmission lever in either neutral or park. Both your owner's manual and the transmission dipstick will tell you which is correct for your car, but here's some information to make it even easier to determine: All GM and Ford products are checked while the car is in the park position. Older Chrysler models are checked in neutral, except for most of their front-wheel-drive cars, which are checked in "park." Most imports also are checked in "park."

2. Your car's engine must be idling when you check the automatic transmission's fluid level, another instruction you'll see printed on the dipstick. This is because the transmission is operated hydraulically, that is, with fluid under pressure.

3. Withdraw the transmission dipstick and wipe it clean with a paper towel. Return the dipstick to the tube, making sure it goes all the way in.

4. Once again, withdraw the dipstick and read the level. Be sure to look at both sides of the dipstick because there's a tendency to get "splash readings." Car owners frequently misread the level of transmission fluid, so I recommend testing the dipstick several times until you get a consistent reading. If the reading continues to differ, believe the reading on the lower side.

5. If you need to add transmission fluid, the type required by your car will be printed on the dipstick. Using a small-mouthed funnel, add fluid directly into the same tube that houses the dipstick. For GM and Chrysler vehicles, the dipsticks usually call for Dexron. Ford may suggest Mercon or Dexron. (These are type names, not brand names.) Refer to your owner's manual for its specification. As fluids have improved, you might see types such as Dexron II. Go with the higher number since it indicates an improved product.

6. There has to be a reason if the fluid level went down, so check for leaks. If none are apparent, take the car to the repair shop because other conditions may cause the level to go down and a skilled auto technician can diagnose the problem.

I like teaching people about transmission fluid because it feels good to trust your own judgment about your car and transmission fluid is easy to evaluate. I'm not just saying this because transmissions are my specialty; maintenance this basic really can boost your self-confidence as you learn to care for your vehicle.

Washer Solvent

Nowhere is the "cleanliness is next to godliness" rule more true than when we're talking about the windshield. Nothing is more dangerous than driving blind because you can't see through the dirt on your windshield, especially if you live in a climate where you face snow and sludge spraying up from the road. On a basic winter day in Pittsburgh, where I live, I might end up cleaning the windshield every mile or so as I drive. That's a good way to run through a lot of washer solvent.

Checking and adding washer solvent is so simple it's senseless to pay another person top dollar to do it for you. Open the hood, locate the solvent reservoir (it will be marked), lift the cap, and pour in the washer solvent. Fill the washer solvent tank only three-quarters of the way. This will allow for any expansion.

You can buy jugs of washer solvent in any grocery store, drugstore, repair shop, or parts store, and often it's on sale super cheap. I recommend that you buy several jugs, and keep one in the trunk at all times so you're never caught empty.

Never substitute plain water for washer solvent, especially in cold climates, because it will freeze. And don't put in dish detergent because it will leave a film that reflects light at night. Some people substitute radiator antifreeze, but this can damage your washer system and, if it leaks, ruin your car's paint job to boot. Stick to the recommended solvent.

Coolant

I've heard a lot of people say they'd change the coolant on their own, but they're never sure how much to add. The solution to that dilemma is an antifreeze tester, available at auto parts stores for just a few dollars. It's a device like a syringe, and its hose is long enough to insert in the radiator to suck up some coolant. A chamber at the top of the tester holds some colored balls. According to the number of balls that float, you'll know to what temperature your cooling system is protected. (The tester is printed with a chart to explain the floating balls.)

Coolant should be warm but not hot when you extract the sample, so run the engine for a few minutes before inserting the antifreeze tester. For instructions on how to add coolant, see Chapter 6.

The Undercarriage

If you think snow and sludge do a number on your windshield, you ought to see what is does to areas underneath your car. Salt from the road crews plays havoc on the exposed parts of the undercarriage. Cars from the 1960s and 1970s had such severe rust damage that frames would rust to eggshell fragility, but metals have improved and frames of later-model cars now hold up longer.

Over time, salt buildup causes deterioration of the fuel lines, exhaust system, brake lines, and the cables that operate the parking brake. Steel lines that carry transmission fluid to the radiator for cooling frequently leak due to rust, as do some of the steel transmission pans. I can't stress strongly enough the importance of hosing off the undercarriage each time it's exposed to salt. If winter temperatures prevent you from doing this at home, take the car through a car wash that sprays underneath.

The Body

Cars are frequently seen as such status symbols that people take elaborate care to wash and wax the exteriors. But you should do this for more than just looks. A good wax job before winter will protect the finish from snow, ice, and salt. When summer rolls around again, put on another heavy coat of wax to protect the finish from the sun. Most people don't realize it's more important to protect your car's finish from the sun than it is to protect it from winter elements. Some colors fade more than others, but all paint is at risk from prolonged sun exposure, and the wax is an invaluable guard against damage.

Maintaining a Smooth Ride—Mile After Mile

So far we've talked about maintenance related to cleanliness, but there's also the kind that falls under the heading "Diligence." Be alert to these conditions and you'll save yourself hundreds of dollars in unnecessary expenses.

Tire Rotation

Repair shops vary in their suggested methods for rotating tires, so while I am presenting one method here, you should also consult your owner's

Common tire rotation pattern
front

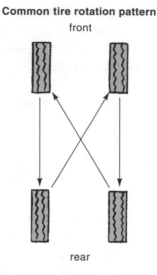

rear

manual and auto technician to see if they have a special recommendation for your car. Tire rotation should be done every 5,000 miles. Failure to follow that schedule will result in two tires wearing out faster than the other two, and you'll get stuck in a cycle of replacing two tires at a time instead of a matching set of four. With proper rotation, all the tires wear evenly and last longer.

Standard tire rotation pattern:

✔ Front tires move straight back (left front to left rear; right front to right rear).

✔ Back tires move forward *and* cross over (left back to right front; right back to left front).

Cars usually come with a small donut spare, but some people prefer to replace it with a full-size tire. If you have a full-size spare, include it in the regularly scheduled tire rotation. A five-wheel tire rotation is different, and you'll want to choose the pattern specifically designed for your car and tires. Consult your owner's manual or tire repair specialist.

Battery Maintenance

We already covered cleaning battery terminals, but older model batteries require you to add water to them regularly as well. (New models are "maintenance-free.") If you have an older model battery, be sure to keep water at the proper level. If the water level gets too low, then the battery won't hold a charge, and continued operation with a low water level will ruin it. If your battery requires water it's a task you can complete yourself, but be very careful as you add the water to the cells because of the acid inside. First remove the caps from each of the six cells and look for the ring that shows where the water level should be. Years ago manufacturers recommended you use distilled water, but that's no longer required; just go ahead and use regular tap water and fill each cell up to the ring.

Cleaning the Radiator

A dirty radiator core cuts down on the air flow through the radiator's honeycomb design. Occasionally check for debris and dried up insect carcasses, especially after a long road trip.

The best way to clean a radiator is to blow it with air. Repair shops can spray it with compressed air, but if your vacuum cleaner at home has reversible hoses, you can blow off the bugs with direct force. If you don't own a vacuum with this feature, hose the radiator clean or pick the bugs off by hand or with a soft brush. Never use a wire brush or a screwdriver.

Chassis Lubrication

In case you're wondering what a chassis is, the simplest explanation is that it's a car with the body removed. It has lots of moving parts, such as steering linkage and ball joints, around the front end and steering, and all of them benefit from lubrication. Neglect this important maintenance procedure and parts wear out very quickly—an abuse I find absolutely inexcusable.

Big, Beautiful Bugs

When my sons were in junior high, they were assigned a project for science class: collect and label an assortment of insects. Unfortunately, neither one had great study habits, and it wasn't until the day before the project was due that they decided to get started. Since it was already late autumn, most of the bugs in Pennsylvania, where we lived, had either left or died, so after delivering yet another lecture about the virtues of being a good student, I took them to my repair shop and one by one we checked the radiators of every car there. My sons found some excellent insect specimens. In fact, one car had just returned from Arizona, so they even had a few exotic bugs, all dried to perfection courtesy of the radiators. Both boys got As on their science project.

Lube jobs are a must on older cars, but newer models have sealed components, so extensive lubing isn't necessary. Read your owner's manual for specifications as to when and how often your car requires lubing. If you determine that your car needs lubrication, you'll have to gather the appropriate equipment.

You will need:

floor jack and jack stands

grease cartridges

grease gun (a tool that forces heavy grease into an area that has a grease fitting to accept it)

owner's manual (for locating parts)

spray can of white lithium grease (available at auto parts stores)

1. Safely jack up your car.

2. Insert a grease cartridge into the grease gun and lubricate the mechanisms listed in your owner's manual. You'll find that a grease gun is very similar to the kind of tool you use to apply caulking around your home.

3. Be sure to lubricate all the hinges on the car, which are frequently neglected. Use the spray can of white lithium grease to lube the door hinges, hood hinges, trunk hinges, and headlight doors if your car has them. And don't forget the hinges on the glove compartment door.

Winterizing or Summerizing Your Car

Every time autumn leaves change colors or spring flowers bloom, you'll see advertisements for "winterizing" and "summerizing" your car. Because the seasons are so different you might think procedures for these "-izings" would be too, but would you believe preparing a car for winter and preparing one for summer involve basically the same steps? They include four basic checks.

Engine Check

Cold weather causes starting problems, so car manufacturers recommend a prewinter check to make sure the engine starts the season at peak performance. But the engine has to run at its best during the summer too, when it is subjected to high temperatures, so schedule a tune-up for your early-model car or a performance check for your later-model vehicle.

Hose and Belt Check

Hoses and belts should be checked to prevent breakdowns in low temperatures, since a broken hose means leaking antifreeze and that means being stranded in bad weather. In summer, a weak hose just might burst if it's exposed to extreme heat.

A broken belt can stop the water pump or the alternator. Lack of a water pump during the summer will exacerbate the risk of overheating, and a stopped alternator in winter increases your odds of a drained battery.

Antifreeze Check

Antifreeze must be checked in the winter to verify that the cooling system is protected against low temperatures. But in the summer it's equally important to have the proper antifreeze mix in cars with air conditioners to prevent overheating. So it's the same check but for different reasons.

Transmission Check

Rocking or spinning tires when you're stuck in a snowdrift can be devastating to a transmission generating enough heat to melt parts. But summer heat affects the transmission too. If temperatures are extreme and you drive long distances, or if you're towing a boat or trailer, it's possible for a transmission to get so hot that it slips or experiences erratic shifting. Extreme overheating also causes the transmission to blow fluid out of a vent and then you're stranded, so before both seasons check the transmission's condition and fluid level.

Storing a Car

I'm talking about serious storage here, six months or longer. Whether it's because you're traveling for an extended period of time or you've decided to retire the car and wait for it to become a classic, storage is serious business. Unless you want to return to a depreciated piece of property, you should follow these steps.

1. Store the vehicle in a cool, dry place with no access for insects or animals. Rodents will feast on a car's interiors and wires.

2. Clean and wax the exterior. If it's been driven in salt, be sure to hose off the undercarriage. Use a dressing (purchased at the auto parts store) on any exterior vinyl.

3. Change the engine oil to ensure there's no moisture trapped in it.

4. Lubricate the chassis; vehicles that sit for a long time tend to rust.

5. Adjust the antifreeze to ensure proper temperature protection for the duration of the car's storage.

6. Squirt engine oil in each cylinder where the spark plug screws in. Without motion and without lubrication, it's possible for the pistons to seize.

7. Disconnect the positive battery terminal to eliminate the risk of fire caused by an electrical short.

8. Put the car up on blocks so the tires don't develop flat spots.

9. Have a full tank of gas to discourage condensation.

Once you're ready to take the car out of storage, reconnect the battery, run the car for about 100 miles on the highway, and then change the engine oil. Your car's now ready for regular use.

Ignore this prescribed schedule and you'll end up with a rapidly deteriorating car on the fast track to a used car lot, where, by the way, you will take a considerable loss on its trade-in value.

The other option is to follow a maintenance schedule and enjoy a car that offers dependable transportation for as long as you wish to keep it. And come trade-in time, you'll have people waiting in line to snap up this exceptional value. Regular maintenance makes all the difference.

It Was a Dark and Stormy Night: Handling Hazards on the Highway

Every car owner dreams of a vehicle that never has a problem, one that purrs contentedly along the highway, ever dependable, trustworthy, and true. You'd visit repair shops only for a routine maintenance check, and once you pulled out of the shop, you'd head straight for the road that leads to the end of the rainbow.

Granted, it's a lovely dream, but real life is filled with dilemmas and difficulties and you can't always depend on the motor club to bail you out. If right now, today, you experienced some emergency situation, something like a flat tire or loss of brakes, could you depend entirely on your own ingenuity to get yourself and your vehicle back on the road?

Sure, some of you might be thinking that since you belong to the motor club, you can skip this chapter, but are you aware that during peak problem times, such as below-zero weather, the motor club might have a waiting list several *hours* long? Are you prepared to sit on the highway for the better part of the afternoon until the cavalry comes to your rescue? I say it makes good safety sense to sock away a little knowledge, and that way you won't always have to rely on the kindness of strangers if you find yourself in a bind.

Assembling an Emergency Kit

T he Boy Scout credo is to always be prepared, so take a tip from the scouts and assemble an emergency kit for your car. I refer to items from the kit as I talk about various emergency situations; so invest some money and you'll be paid back with confidence and peace of mind.

The kit won't take up much room, and it doesn't have to be fancy either. Many of these items are probably lying around your house. Start with an old duffel bag or a diaper bag and add the following items:

- ✔ small throw rug (for kneeling on the ground during repairs)
- ✔ work gloves
- ✔ 2 bread wrappers and 4 rubber bands
- ✔ 1 large standard screwdriver
- ✔ 1 pair of pliers
- ✔ spray can of penetrating oil
- ✔ set of battery jumper cables
- ✔ wheel chock
- ✔ emergency flares
- ✔ large flashlight and extra batteries
- ✔ rubber hammer
- ✔ folding shovel (or a short-handled shovel)
- ✔ 1 roll of mechanic's wire

✔ 4-way tire wrench

✔ funnel

✔ old shower curtain (for a ground covering if you have to crawl under the car)

✔ old scarf (for emergency hose repairs) and an old belt (the kind you use to hold up your pants)

✔ bag of cat box filler or rock salt

✔ cigarette lighter

✔ plastic jug of water

✔ basic first-aid pack

✔ fluorescent safety vest (to wear if you have to repair a car on the side of the road)

✔ dried fruit or nonperishable food in case you ever get stranded, along with a blanket to ward off cold weather

Safety Guidelines

Now that your emergency kit is securely in the trunk, sit back and enjoy the ride. Who needs the cavalry when you've got such a prepared and confident driver at the wheel? But keep in mind that not everything you need to remain safe fits neatly in a kit. I'm talking about common sense here. If you break down, follow these general guidelines for personal safety:

1. Try to move the car completely off the road.

2. Never stand near the edge of the highway while checking the car.

3. At night, turn on the flashers to signal your need for help. During the day, raise the hood and tie a white cloth on the antenna or door handle.

4. Set out flares, and if you have to repair the car at night, wear a fluorescent safety vest.

5. While you wait for help to arrive, stay inside your car with the windows up and the door locked. Never accept a ride from a passing motorist.

6. Devise a plan for getting assistance *before* you face a crisis. Carry a cellular phone or carry a cardboard sign for your windshield (preprinted ones are available at the auto parts store) asking motorists to call the police. If you have no other option, wait for daylight and walk to a phone, being sure to wear your fluorescent safety vest whenever you leave the car.

Flat Tires

Murphy's Law has most tires going flat when you have a deadline to meet at work or else when you're dressed in your best clothes (frequently, it's a combination of both), so if you can spare the time you're better off waiting for the motor club. After all, changing a flat is hard, dirty work, and it doesn't really prove anything to do it if you can avoid the task.

However, 11 percent of the 2.4 million service calls made each year to the AAA are for flat tires. That suggests a heck of a waiting list if you're suddenly one of the 264,000, so invest some time to learn how to change a flat on your own. And by the way, the very worst time to learn how to change a flat is when you're already stuck on the side of the road! Better to schedule a little drill in your driveway so you're ready if the real thing ever strikes—and invite an experienced friend, auto technician, even your mom or dad to supervise, just to make sure you're doing it right.

Where you are when the flat tire occurs has a lot to do with how involved the job will be. If it's at home, great; getting help will be easier and you've got the added bonus of safely changing the tire away from moving traffic. Unfortunately, statistics show that most flat tires happen in The Middle of Nowhere (consult your map), and you absolutely must get the car to a safe, level spot before proceeding with repairs.

Steer the car to the shoulder of the road and pull as far to the right as possible. If the road is unpaved, be sure to stop on a solid surface. Whether the car is in your driveway or on a shoulder, the surface must be perfectly flat because on a slope, even a slight one, the car might just roll off the jack once it's in the air.

Drive the car only if you are not near a safe area for changing the tire. Definitely don't attempt to drive the car any substantial distance with a flat tire, because you will not only ruin the tire, you will also ruin the wheel. Of course, if you have to choose between ruining a tire and driving until you find a safe spot, there really is no choice. Personal safety must come first.

If you have to change the tire on the road, turn on your flashers and open the hood to alert other drivers that your car is in an emergency situation. Then open your trunk and gather the tools you'll need. Take out the jack and the spare tire, which should be fully inflated because you've been checking it regularly during your scouting trips. Also remove your emergency kit.

Don't be embarrassed if you have to consult your owner's manual to locate where the jack is stored; it changes from model to model and that can get tricky. Instructions for using the jack properly should be printed on the inside of the trunk lid; you absolutely *must* read them before you attempt to operate the jack. All cars have specific spots on the car where the jack should be used, and you're placing yourself in real danger if you attach the jack incorrectly.

One more tip about jacks before we move on: If you purchase a used car, test the jack before you leave the car lot. Some used car lots have a tendency to play "musical car jacks," and you just might end up with one that wasn't designed for your vehicle. You really don't want to discover this after you've broken down on the side of the road.

Now you're ready to open your emergency kit and pull out the old throw rug so you have something to kneel on, pull on the work gloves, and finally get out the chock. Few cars' jacking equipment come with a chock, that is, a rubber wedge to help keep the car from sliding as you change the flat tire. You can make a wooden chock by diagonally cutting a solid 6 × 6 × 6-inch block, which will leave you with a triangular-shaped wedge of wood. If worse comes to worse, use a large rock.

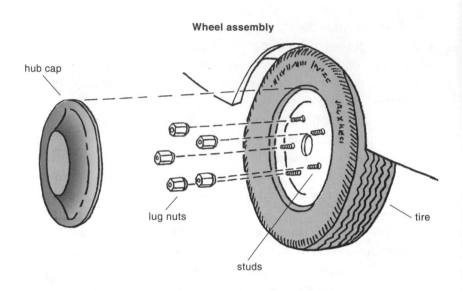

Wheel assembly

hub cap

lug nuts

studs

tire

Place the chock under the wheel diagonally across from the flat tire (for example, if the back left tire is flat, the chock would go under the right front tire).

Next, put on your parking brake and move the automatic transmission lever to the "park" position. If you have a manual transmission, put the lever in first gear. You are now ready to safely change the flat tire.

You will need:

standard screwdriver

lug wrench or 4-way lug wrench

penetrating oil

tire jacking equipment

spare tire or donut spare

rubber hammer (optional)

1. Using a large screwdriver from the emergency kit or the tapered end of the lug wrench, remove the hubcap. If your car has alloy wheels, you'll have to remove the lug nut cover. If your car has a safety feature that locks the wheels in place, then you'll need the wheel lock tool as well.

Flat Tire Fashions

A s we've already established, a flat tire will happen when you're wearing your best outfit, so I've come up with some tips for keeping clothes clean. We've already mentioned the work gloves and a rug to kneel on, but the areas most likely to be sweat-stained and soiled after changing a flat tire are your shirtsleeves. I suggested keeping two clean, plastic bread wrappers and four rubber bands in your emergency kit. This is where they come into play. Cut the closed end of the bread bags and slide one bag over each arm. Secure at the wrists and upper arms with the rubber bands. While it might not be the most fashionable accessory in your wardrobe, your sleeves will still be clean once the flat tire's fixed.

2. Loosen all lug nuts using the lug wrench at one end of the jack handle. For better leverage, purchase a 4-way lug wrench. Loosen lug nuts a turn or two *before* you jack the car into the air because the lug nuts will be tight and the weight of the car will offer additional leverage to loosen them. Trying to break them loose once the car's in the air would take so much strength you just might end up forcing the car off the jack. If you have trouble loosening the lug nuts, take the can of penetrating oil from the emergency kit and give the lug nuts a spray.

3. Fit the jack underneath the car according to the jack's instructions. Raise the car until the flat tire is 2 or 3 inches off the ground.

4. Remove the loosened lug nuts and the wheel. Place the lug nuts in the upside-down hubcap for safekeeping.

Loosening Lug Nuts

You don't have to be superman to loosen lug nuts; anyone with normal strength should be able to handle it. But many of today's state-of-the-art auto technicians use air guns to tighten everything, and overtightening of lug nuts has become a serious problem.

Whenever anyone performs a service on your car requiring removal of the wheel—for instance, brake work or tire replacement—request loudly and clearly that you want all lug nuts *hand-tightened.* If the lug nuts are hand-tightened, you can be assured you'll be able to *hand-loosen* them too.

5. Fit the spare onto the car and replace the lug nuts, making sure each one is finger-tight. Remember that the *tapered* side of the lug nut always goes against the wheel.

6. Lower the car to the ground and use the lug wrench to tighten the lug nuts one at a time. It doesn't matter which one you start with, but tighten the lug nuts in a crisscross pattern (if you traced it, the outline would be a five-point star) until they're all secure. (See illustration on page 111.)

7. Put the hubcap or lug nut cover on the wheel and gently tap it into place with the rubber hammer from your emergency kit. If you don't have a rubber hammer, toss the hubcap or wheel cover in the trunk and put it on properly once you're home. Losing the hubcap or wheel cover will only add insult to injury after dealing with the aggravation of a flat tire.

8. Put your jack and the wheel chock back in their proper place so they'll be available for the next emergency, and put the flat

Numbered lug nuts

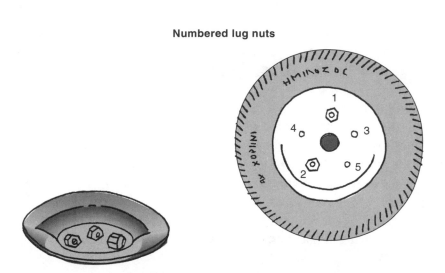

tire in the trunk. Be sure to take it to a tire repair shop *immedi-ately*. It's easy to forget that part.

The Spare Tire and Other Options

Now that you have successfully completed the tire change and loaded your emergency kit back into the trunk, there are a few things you should know about your spare tire. Most cars come equipped with a donut spare, a smaller tire designed to save space (and cost, I'm sure). Donuts are designed for emergency situations only and should be used only to get you to a facility where you can repair or replace the flat tire. Never try to fudge and drive long distances with the donut; it has very little tread and a maximum life of about fifty miles. Also be sure to observe the weight limit listed on the side of the donut, and if your car has a donut on it, don't tow anything. If you frequently travel long distances or tow a trailer or boat, you might consider just pitching the donut spare and investing in an extra wheel and full-size tire.

Some of you who browse the auto parts store might be familiar with an aerosol tire inflator that contains a substance to stop the leak and inflate the tire. It may be a good item to keep around as a last-ditch emergency repair when changing the flat tire is out of the question due to

Avoiding the Jack Jigsaw Puzzle

I have one little tip that may make you feel like an idiot, but it could turn out to be extremely helpful. Some of those car jacks are packed in like some kind of geometric experiment from NASA, so take a Polaroid snapshot of the jack equipment while it's neatly packed and keep it in the trunk for future reference. You'll already be cranky from changing the flat tire; you don't want to top off a bad day by having to play jigsaw puzzle with the jack when it's time to put it away.

safety concerns. But only use it as a last resort because the product has some drawbacks. Some brands contain flammable gases. Also, they're designed to stop only small leaks, not blowouts or problems with the tire valve. And as an auto technician, I will tell you that tire repair facilities positively hate these products, because they fill the tire with a gooey substance that has to be cleaned before the flat tire can be repaired. The bottom line is: You're better off changing the tire.

My final advice about flat tires is to be realistic. If you know deep in your heart and soul that you just aren't cut out to change flat tires, at least have a backup plan. A cellular phone in the car may be an added expense, but it's great for calling in the cavalry.

Dead Battery

Few things are as distressing as the slow cranking and groaning sounds from a dying battery. You might have enough energy to operate lights and accessories, but the greedy starter requires more power than the dying battery can muster, and your car simply won't start.

Buying Jumper Cables

When you invest in jumper cables, buy a set of decent ones. Occasionally you see them in discount stores for $5 or $6, but I always caution people to be careful with the cheap cables: Sometimes after one good jump the cables are shot. Obviously you don't have to buy the really heavy ones similar to those the repair shops use, but it makes sense to buy cables that will last. Be sure the alligator clips on the ends of the cables work with both top-loaded and side-loaded terminals. A good set at the auto parts store will run about $18 to $20.

So what do you do? Let's assume you can't call the motor club, or that their waiting list is longer than your patience. Now would be a good time to know how to use a set of battery jumper cables. Once again, practice this procedure before you have to perform it in a real emergency. I highly advise against attempting to jump a battery if you don't know how to do it properly. Take this simple test if you aren't sure: Do you have to ask what "negative" and "positive" mean when it comes to the battery terminal? If you do have to ask, leave this job for the pros.

Jumping a battery has the same effect as physically borrowing someone else's battery and putting it in your car—without actually having to do that, of course, since it would be pretty inconvenient. Jumper cables are two separate heavy wires with alligator clips on the ends. One has red handles and the other has black so you don't get them mixed up. I think a set of quality jumper cables in the trunk is the mark of a genuine Educated Car Owner.

Before you get started, pull out your owner's manual and read what it has to say about jumping the battery. With later-model computer-controlled cars you have to be extremely careful, so read the information over and over until you completely understand it. If the manual advises against using jumper cables on your model car, then don't experiment. It looks like you're just going to have to wait for professional help.

Okay, let's say you've read your owner's manual and determined it can stand a battery jump. The first thing you have to do is round up a good, charged battery to borrow from. Maybe you've got a good neighbor or a kindly passing motorist has stopped to help. If they're concerned the jump will drain their good battery, you can assure them it only takes the same amount of energy needed to start their own car. The only exception to this is if the car with the dead battery got that way because of a bad starter drawing way too much electricity from the battery. But even if it takes more energy to start your car, the battery in the good car will recharge itself just by running the engine.

Understanding that, most drivers will let you jump from their batteries if you're armed with jumper cables and a cool, confident look of know-how. Assuming you've gotten this far, it's time to jump the battery.

You will need:

1 pair of jumper cables

car with a charged battery

1. Park the car with the good battery close to but not touching yours, nose to nose or side by side. Both cars should be turned off.

2. Connect the red-handled cable to the positive battery terminal of the good battery. Connect the other red end to the positive terminal of your dead battery. To ward against mistakes, the terminals will be marked very clearly with a + for positive and a − for negative. The positive terminal post is also usually larger than the negative one.

3. Connect one end of the black cable to the negative terminal on the good battery and the other end to a ground on the car with the dead battery. The ground must be a heavy steel part, such as a steel bracket on the alternator or power steering.

Connecting the Negative Terminal to a Ground

There's a reason you want to connect the negative terminal to a ground on the car with the dead battery. Batteries tend to form gas inside, a condition that worsens when they are dead. You might produce a spark as you connect the jumper cables from the good battery to the negative terminal, which could cause the battery to explode.

I caused a battery to explode once, in my younger days. It was very cold and snowy, and I couldn't find a good ground on the car I was jumping so I impatiently connected it to the negative terminal. It sparked and *boom!* The battery blew up. Fortunately I wasn't hurt, but it really made a believer out of me. I never took the easy way out again, and whenever I teach classes I always emphasize the connection to a ground and *not* to the negative terminal.

I don't say all this to frighten you. I just want to point out that it is a safe procedure *if* you follow the rules.

4. Now that the jumper cables are connected properly, start the engine of the car with the good battery. Then start the engine of your car, the one with the dead battery. Let both cars run for about five minutes before disconnecting the cables.

5. When you disconnect the cables, reverse the procedure: Disconnect the negative cable first, starting with the ground. Then disconnect the positive jumper cables.

Jumper cable connections

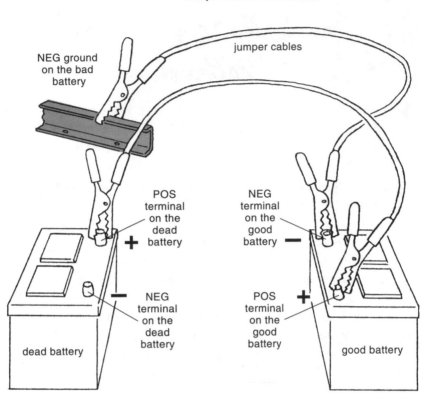

NEG ground
on the bad
battery

jumper cables

POS
terminal
on the
dead
battery

+

NEG
terminal
on the
good
battery

—

NEG
terminal
on the
dead
battery

—

POS
terminal
on the
good
battery

+

dead battery

good battery

6. Fold up the cables and return them safely to your emergency kit, so they're ready and waiting for the next crisis.

I have just one more point I'd like to make: Don't just jump the dead battery, figure out why it died in the first place. Unless it was something obvious, like you forgot to turn off your headlights when you parked, you can expect a repeat of the dead battery episode. If you drained the battery by mistake, driving the car will recharge it, but all other possibilities should be checked out by your auto technician. If you can't get your car to the service shop immediately, be sure to park it in a place that leaves you access to the hood, just in case you have to jump the battery again.

Relying on the Kindness of Strangers

I f I could arrange it, I'd start a national "Honor Your Auto Mechanic Week," or even a "Take Your Mechanic to Lunch Day." You'd be amazed at how many customers get irate when a mechanic is just trying to do his job, but these very same people would readily accept the help of a stranger if their cars were broken down on the side of the road. Don't get me wrong, I'm not knocking the kindness of strangers. But I strongly caution you not to take the advice of every last person who offers, whether it's a well-meaning neighbor or a self-proclaimed expert who just happened by.

Once my car broke down, and as I waited for the tow truck on the side of the road, a steady string of well-intentioned motorists stopped to offer assistance. Now, I am an auto technician, so I knew exactly what was wrong with the car, and even though I kept repeating I was fine and would prefer to wait for the motor club, the very situation made a lot of these samaritans sudden experts, tugging at wires and suggesting all kinds of impossible things that might be wrong. I finally had to be rude and send them on their way. The point is that while their motives were altruistic, they weren't qualified or experienced enough to be fiddling around under the hood.

If you find yourself in a similar situation, I suggest you politely but firmly keep people away from your car. If they really want to help, they can place a phone call to the motor club for you or notify emergency assistance.

Overheating

The next time you're driving in very slow-moving traffic on a stifling hot day, pay close attention to the sides of the road. Odds are good you'll be looking at a string of cars on the berm, hoods open, steam pouring out of the engine area, and, as the crowning detail, a forlorn, perplexed, and perspiring car owner nearby watching the scene.

Maybe this sounds way too familiar; maybe *you* were the perplexed and perspiring car owner. Don't feel too bad—you're in good company. Even the best of us sometimes forget that slow-moving traffic and extreme temperatures cause a perfectly healthy car to overheat. According to the National Car Care Council, overheating is the number-one cause of roadside breakdowns.

If your car is already spewing steam from under the hood, you've reached the overheating danger zone. Your choices are either to pull the car to the side of the road and let it cool down, or keep on driving and overheat completely. Unless you're a masochist, you should choose to pull your car to the side of the road.

Open the hood so air can circulate and dissipate the heat. After the engine cools down—which takes at least twenty minutes—you can continue your journey, but take some precautions to prevent a repeat performance of the overheating:

✔ Roll down the windows and make the rest of the trip sans air conditioner. Don't cave in and turn on the a/c, no matter how hot you get! The air conditioner puts a tremendous drag on the engine, robs it of power, steals from the mileage, and adds to the heat.

✔ If you're already driving without air conditioning and the temperature still shows high or the red warning light stays lit on the dash, turn on the heater. Yes, you read that correctly: *Turn on the heater.* This allows coolant to circulate in a larger area by going through the heater core, and it should help cool down the car.

✔ Do not let the engine idle when you're sitting in traffic. By *idle,* I mean the fuel system is feeding just enough fuel into the engine to keep it running when there is no load on it. So when you are sitting in traffic for prolonged periods without moving at all, put the transmission lever in neutral and step lightly on the accelerator. Not too much, you understand, just enough to increase the RPMs of the engine. This will cause the fan to turn faster and the water pump will pump faster, causing the cooling system to work much better.

If you've done all that and the car *still* overheats, roll up your shirtsleeves and head for the emergency kit in your trunk.

You will need:

rag

jug of water

old scarf and clothing belt (to use if the hose is split)

NOTE: An overheated car can cause serious injury if you attempt to remove the radiator cap immediately after it has overheated. For safe instructions see Chapter 4, "Radiator Cap Removal."

1. Get the car to a safe area off the road, if possible, and allow it to cool down.

2. When the car has cooled sufficiently, use a rag to remove the radiator cap, following the directions in Chapter 4.

3. Start the car's engine and add water directly to the radiator.

4. Replace the radiator cap to the locked position.

5. If overheating caused a hose to split, use the old scarf and clothing belt to jury-rig a repair. (See illustration on page 120.) Tightly wrap the scarf around the split hose, then tighten the old belt around the scarf. This should slow the leak enough to let you limp into a repair shop.

Replace the lost fluid from the cooling system with the proper mixture of water and antifreeze as soon as possible. And remember, just cooling down the engine and adding water is not the solution to an overheated engine. You have to determine why it overheated in the first place and then solve the problem.

Temporary repair of a split hose

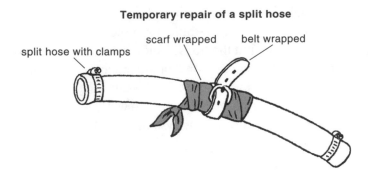

Flooded Engine

We already discussed the futility of pumping the gas pedal when you realize the engine is flooded. You have to allow the liquid gasoline to evaporate and the spark plugs to dry out, so sing a song, watch the scenery, meditate if you have to. Just don't get impatient and pump the gas pedal or you'll only prolong your problem. In three to five minutes, depending on how bad the flood was, the engine should start. If it doesn't then the liquid gasoline might have soaked the plugs, and you'll have to clean or replace them. While spark plug replacement used to be a simple repair, in some of today's cars you can't even reach them, so you may want to rely on a professional for the fix.

The best solution to a flooded engine is patience on the part of the driver, but there are a couple of things you can do by way of damage control:

✔ If you have a carbureted car and the engine floods, after waiting for a few minutes, put the gas pedal all the way to the floor and hold it there while cranking the starter to get maximum air coming in.

✔ Also keep the gas pedal to the floor if your car has a fuel injection system, but for a different reason. This sends a message to the car's computer that the engine is flooded and the computer will automatically adjust to let in less fuel. See, in some cases cars are smarter than people!

Frozen Car Doors and Locks

We all know the hazards of driving in snow and ice, but one of the most exasperating winter conditions happens before you even get in your car. I'm talking about that really frustrating moment when it's ten degrees F, you're late for work, and you can't get in the car because the doors are frozen shut.

Actually, there are two different ways this happens. Either the lock is frozen or the door itself is frozen shut, a result of moisture or condensation that has collected there and solidified. If you find yourself the victim of this infuriating problem, there are a few dos and don'ts designed to get you inside. First, let's deal with the don'ts.

While you might be tempted to haul off with a sledgehammer and break a window, resist the urge. The ice has a lot more stamina than you do, and any attempts to force open the door, either by pounding, tugging, or using a screwdriver or crowbar, only will damage the car.

You also may think you can melt the ice by pouring hot water over the frozen parts. Unfortunately, the hot water will cool and freeze a lot faster than the ice will melt, so you'll be stuck with even more ice on the door than before. Also, pouring hot water on a cold window just might cause the glass to shatter, and then you'll really be in a rotten mood.

Try the simplest solutions first. If the lock is frozen, try the old heated-key trick. Hold the door key directly over a flame. A cigarette lighter works best because you can keep a steady flame longer, but a candle or matches work too. After the key heats, stick it in the lock, repeating the process as many times as it takes to thaw the ice.

If your car is close enough to an electrical outlet, or if you can run an extension cord, I find a hair dryer to be an ideal way to thaw out a frozen door. Sure, you might get some strange looks from the neighbors, but you'll be in your car in a matter of minutes.

And don't forget the obvious solutions too. Check out the other doors first. Often wind direction or the way your car is parked exposes only one door to the elements, and the other doors might open easily. You even can crawl in the hatchback if you have to. Again, not the most dignified way to start your day, but at least you'll be in your car.

To save wear and tear on your doors (and your dignity), I suggest you invest in a few of the products designed to prevent frozen locks in the first place. Some come in aerosol containers, and the mixture of alcohol and lubricant will prevent another episode.

And one last commonsense tip: When you wash your car in the winter, be sure to do it in a heated garage.

Frozen Cooling System

Did you ever tempt fate by betting that you'd have enough antifreeze in your cooling system and that the temperature wouldn't really go as low as predicted? I'm sure we've all gambled and won on occasion, but what do you do when you're wrong and the coolant freezes?

If the temperature really drops and the coolant freezes solid, it can crack the engine block, and suddenly you'll be facing an engine replacement costing thousands of dollars. More often the problem isn't so drastic, but you'll still suffer some consequences. The system can freeze enough to paralyze the water pump and make slush in the radiator. If your car starts just fine on a cold morning, but then starts to steam and overheat after you've driven a few miles, chances are very good your coolant is frozen.

You'll have to check to be sure, so raise the hood of the engine and feel the radiator hose. If it remains cold then you're not getting any circulation of coolant. If the temperature dropped and you didn't have a proper level of antifreeze protection, that's the reason for the freezing, although a thermostat that was stuck closed would react the same way.

What should you do if you've allowed your car's cooling system to freeze? I say the first thing you do is name yourself the recipient of the Car Maintenance Negligence Award, because this was one problem you could have prevented very easily. The next thing you do is get the car to a service station, which will involve towing, and keep it inside until the cooling system thaws. Once it does you can add more antifreeze. The whole ordeal will cost you, of course, and just think how easily it could have been avoided. So that you don't face the same costly and embarrassing problem next winter, put a note on your calendar to check your car's temperature protection level each autumn and add the necessary antifreeze.

Loss of Brakes

I have talked about various aspects of brake failure several times in this book, but only because it is such a terrifying experience. Unfortunately, it is also something I can talk about from firsthand knowledge because some years ago my car suffered a complete brake failure. I was going down a hill, picking up speed, and careening toward an intersection. Since I worked with cars, even taught classes about them, you'd think I of all people could resist the urge to panic. Not so, because let me tell you, there aren't enough words in the English language to describe the terror I experienced at that moment. I let critical seconds slip by while I panicked. Finally I wised up and took hold of the situation, putting the transmission in a lower gear to slow it down. My choices were to crash into a grocery store or veer right and hit a large outdoor sign. I chose the sign and steered in that direction, but before I got there my car hit the curb and slowed down. With the help of the technique to be described, I was able to roll to a stop just inches from the road sign. I did several hundred dollars' worth of damage to the undercarriage, but it was worth it because no one got hurt.

The moral of the story is, make the logical part of your brain convince the panicky part to recover quickly because you minimize danger when you calmly follow the right sequence of steps.

1. Rapidly pump the brake pedal. Sometimes this will create enough braking power to slow down or even stop the car.

2. If pumping the pedal doesn't help, it's time to try the transmission. Shift the transmission lever into second and then into first. Your car should slow down. Next, gently apply the parking brake to bring the car to a complete stop.

3. If the car is still moving and it is inevitable that you will hit something, try sideswiping a curb or a wall. An indirect collision is better than one that's head-on.

The good news is complete brake failure is a rarity with today's cars, and vehicles are even designed to give you warnings before the failure becomes extreme. Pay attention to these clues:

- ✔ Soft, mushy brake pedal

- ✔ Brakes that pull to one side when you depress the pedal (indicates loss of brake fluid)

- ✔ Dash light flashing "brakes"

Any of these clues should send you straight to the repair shop to let an expert check out the system.

Engine Stall

A stalling engine sounds like a pesky condition, inconvenient but not actually dangerous. Wrong. In cars with power steering and power brakes, a stalling engine means loss of power to those systems, and suddenly you're in a car that's practically uncontrollable. Even something as simple as drifting into an intersection at slow speed can have catastrophic results. Unfortunately, you can't anticipate a stall, and once you're in it, there's nothing you can do to recover the lost power features, so take preventive measures against a stalling engine by sticking to your maintenance schedule.

I suggest you even take your car to an empty parking lot to get the feel of your brakes and the steering in a stall. Simulate it by shutting off the ignition while you're moving and allowing the car to drift a few feet, and you'll be able to determine how much strength it takes to steer and stop without power assist.

Stuck Horn

Has the horn on your car ever malfunctioned and continued to blare no matter what you did to stop it? Talk about a way to become popular with the neighbors! Once is more than enough for this embarrassing situation, so learn where the horn is located on your car and how to disconnect it if it malfunctions.

The toughest part of this whole assignment is locating the horn. In older cars they're easier to find, but in the newer cars you'd think the manufacturers hid them deliberately. The horn is shaped like a big black snail, and most cars have two of them to create a pleasant two-tone sound. (Economy cars are more likely to have just one horn with an atonal beep.) Check the fender walls, behind the grille, and the side of the radiator. If you still can't find the horn, enlist the help of your favorite mechanic. You'll feel a whole lot better once you see how long it takes him or her to locate the horn.

Once you locate the horn, disconnecting it is a simple matter of pulling the plug, just as you would to disconnect any household appliance. Unplugging the car's horn will be your only contribution to the handling of this emergency, though, because you'll have to leave the repair of whatever caused the horn malfunction to the professionals. The problem may have originated from a loose connection or from a short in the electrical wires, possibly in the steering column. Tracking the cause requires a skilled technician and a lot of time.

If you have a problem with a malfunctioning horn, don't get lazy and think just because you've disconnected it your troubles are over. The horn is one of your car's most important safety features. You use it to alert other drivers and pedestrians and even animals to an emergency situation. In states that require a safety inspection, your car won't pass unless the horn is in working order.

Keys Locked in the Car

This one's guaranteed to raise your blood pressure because not only is it a pain to remedy, but you know you've got only yourself to blame. In the good old days, if you locked your keys in the car, you could get real handy with a coat hanger and pull up the lock. Problem was, car thieves were among the handiest with the hangers, so manufacturers changed the design of the locks. Even the thin metal strips referred to as "slim jims" are a thing of the past. With all the advanced wiring and mecha-

Tooting My Own Horn

Horns hint at the car's personality; for instance, the big luxury cars have mellow, musical horns, while smaller models are stuck with high-pitched yapping that sounds like a hysterical lapdog or honking from a deranged goose. Be aware that you can have your auto technician change the horn in your car if you want a different sound. Some specialty stores even sell car horns that play little tunes, so feel free to experiment if you really despise the horn your car was "born" with. Someone once gave me a horn that played "Come Away with Me, Lucille, in My Merry Oldsmobile." I used it for a while, but the darn thing was so loud and, well, *goofy* that after a few days I finally put the old one back in.

nisms inside the car door, you'd do a lot of damage if you jammed a slim jim between the window glass and door moldings.

So where does that leave you if your mind strays long enough to slam the door shut while the keys are still in the ignition? Your options are:

✔ Take a cab or a bus to your spare set of keys.

✔ Call the car dealer where you purchased the car and have them make a new key.

✔ Call the motor club. Most have experts at unlocking car doors. In fact, I once watched a motor club tech open a locked Beretta inside of sixteen seconds.

✔ As a last resort, or in an emergency, you might consider breaking the car window. Save this one for the real crisis situation though, because window replacement is very expensive.

Some stores sell little key containers attached to magnets that can be hidden somewhere on the outside of your car, for instance, on the under side of a fender. While they are handy, keep in mind that car criminals are getting savvier by the day, and they know to look for those key containers too.

You might be better off devising a system or pattern that will keep you from locking the keys in the car in the first place. I have a friend who used to lock her keys in her car on such a regular basis, people thought it was one of her hobbies. Now she always turns off the car accessories and the engine in the same order, removes the key from the ignition, and won't close the door once she gets out of the car unless she is actually looking at the key in her hand. A little compulsive, maybe, but at least she doesn't get locked out anymore.

Driving in Fog

Driving in fog is stressful and very dangerous, so avoid it if you can. Unfortunately, that's not always possible, and on long road trips you might find yourself driving in and out of regions that specialize in fog. If that's the case, follow these precautions:

 Drive *very* slowly. Visibility may be so bad that you can't see another car or road obstruction until you're practically on top of it. By driving slowly you'll decrease your stopping distance.

 If your car is not equipped with fog lights, use your low beams. The moisture suspended in the air will reflect the light back at you, so if you use high beams you actually make visibility conditions worse.

 If the fog is spotty, take extra precautions as you enter valleys or dips where fog settles. You could suddenly run into a wave of fog and be blinded by it, especially in terrain that features swamps, ponds, or other bodies of water.

 If you find yourself in an area so foggy that visibility drops to zero, pull off the road immediately and wait for the fog to lift. Make sure your blinkers or hazard lights are on for the duration of the time you're stopped, so other drivers are aware of you.

If you live in an area prone to heavy or frequent fogs, you might consider installing fog lights on your car. Installation kits complete with lights and hardware are available at any auto parts store, and they range in price from $40 all the way up to $200. Read the instructions very carefully before you attempt to install these lights. While you might be able to handle the drilling and light installation, actually wiring the lights into your electrical system gets tricky. This might be a job best left to the professionals, although to cut down on the costs you could still bring in the kit you purchased yourself.

Driving in Rain: Hydroplaning

Were you ever driving at a pretty fast clip in a rainstorm when suddenly your car felt as if it were out of control, almost airborne? Chances are good you were hydroplaning. Hydroplaning occurs at high speeds when water gets between the tire and the surface of the road. The tires don't need to be completely bald for this to happen either, just badly worn—another good argument for regular tire rotation and maintenance.

Hydroplaning is pretty scary, and your first instinct might be to slam on the brakes, but avoid that instinct. The better way to deal with hydroplaning is to let the car slow down naturally. It's a lot like driving on snow or ice: Slam on the brakes and you'll find yourself in a skid. Follow the same precautions listed in the next section, "Driving on Snow and Ice."

Driving on Snow and Ice

Some people are so afraid of driving in snow they literally garage the car until the spring thaw. That kind of drastic measure really limits your mobility, so follow these tips for safer snow driving.

✔ Be especially careful of snow or wet conditions at 25 to 30 degrees F. You'll only get half as much traction in wet snow than you'd get on solidly frozen roads at lower temperatures.

✔ Watch high-traffic roads, intersections, and curves, because snow and ice get packed down and even slicker than usual.

✔ Don't lower air pressure in your tires thinking it will give you better traction. Tire inflation already drops one pound for every ten-degree drop in temperature; lowering it on your own can create a tire that's too flat.

✔ When you find yourself driving on snowy or icy areas, start slowly to avoid losing the small amount of traction between the wheels, and the road. Every time you spin those wheels, the snow gets smoother and the traction decreases. If you do start to skid, steer *into* the direction of the skid.

✔ You may not realize it, but cars steer by traction too. Always rotate the steering wheel gently and drive slowly enough going into a turn so you don't have to do any sudden steering moves. Turning creates centrifugal force, and if you combine that with no traction at the front wheels, the result is a sure skid.

✔ Apply brakes by gently tapping on the pedal, about once or twice a second, so you don't break the traction between the wheels and the snow. Remember that stopping in snow could take up to four times the normal stopping distance. If you're driving 20 mph in dry conditions, it might take you anywhere from 25 to 40 feet to stop, so driving in snow at 20 mph means stopping could take almost 200 feet. Keep your eyes on the road far ahead to avoid surprises.

✔ You might have noticed a trend here: Drive gently, brake gently, steer gently. The premise extends to your temper too. Don't sit and stew if you're stuck in the snow, and definitely don't spin your wheels in frustration. Calmly get out of the car, retrieve your emergency kit supplies, and throw a handful of dirt or cat box filler, even an old newspaper, under the rear wheels to create better traction.

✔ The "overdrive" feature is not designed for snowy conditions, so keep the transmission in lower gears.

✔ Keep your trunk's emergency kit well stocked, and keep an extra jug of windshield washer solvent in the car during the winter. Dirty snow splattered up from the wheels of other cars can spell zero visibility for you.

Getting Stuck in Snow, Mud, or Sand

If you've somehow gotten the car so deeply stuck in snow, mud, or sand that it won't move at all, you have only two options that won't damage your car. You can either dig out the wheels or call in the tow truck. Those are the *only* two options I recommend, yet many drivers still think they can get out by racing the engine or rocking the car back and forth from "drive" to "reverse."

In my shop I've had cars towed in with some pretty extensive damage, all because the drivers tried to rock their cars out of snowdrifts. I've seen broken and tangled fan belts, broken timing belts, and plenty of melted transmission parts. In fact, rocking back and forth can generate enough extreme heat to shorten the life span of a brand-new transmission to less than a day. The worst case of Snow Frustration Abuse I ever saw happened to a small front-wheel-drive vehicle. The owner called to request a tow into the shop, and since we were in the middle of a long stretch of snow and cold temperatures I casually asked if he'd been stuck in the snow. His response was just as casual. *A little, nothing major.* Well, when the tow truck returned, the tow driver brought me not only the car but also a bag of car parts he'd collected from underneath the car—which just happened to be stuck in the snow where it had worn two huge ruts from rocking the car. I had to congratulate the guy: He'd rocked the car enough to destroy his final drive and enough for the gears actually to blow a hole through the case.

Don't let your temper or impatience get the best of you when the car gets stuck in the snow, sand, or mud. Take the shovel out of the emergency kit in your trunk and resolve to dig your way out. If that isn't working, call the tow truck, because the cost of a tow is a mere pittance compared to the price of rebuilding a transmission. After digging your way out of the mud or sand, I suggest you have the wheels pulled so the parts can be cleaned and lubricated. Those kinds of elements can gum up the works and cause more problems down the line. (I once got so stuck in South Carolina that, for the next few years, every time I pulled a wheel off my GTO I saw that red Carolina soil.)

Running Out of Gas

I always say running out of gas once should teach you a lesson that lasts a lifetime, and yet some people still do it on a regular basis. They insist their cars still can make it another twenty miles once the gas gauge reads empty—and I know even bigger gamblers who drive in cars where the gas gauge is broken completely—but I strongly advise against these little games. Running out of gas puts you in a stupid, unnecessary, and even dangerous situation; avoid it by always refueling when the car gets down to a quarter tank. This not only prevents running out of gas, but it's a lot better for your fuel system too. In fuel-injected cars, the fuel pump is in the gas tank, and it shouldn't be run dry. Also, running on the very last dregs of gasoline encourages sediment or moisture from the bottom of the gas tank to be sucked into the fuel lines. The debris can slip past a filter and cause plenty of problems if it reaches the carburetor or fuel-injection system.

Call for help or walk to the nearest gas station (never, ever hitch a ride from a passing motorist) and use the funnel from your emergency kit to fill your tank with enough gas to get your car to a proper filling station. If you have a fuel-injection system or a computer-controlled carburetor fuel system, the engine will start right up after you add gasoline. Not so in the old days when you had to pour a little gasoline directly into the carburetor to prime it after running out of gas.

Dragging Parts from the Undercarriage

Did you ever have a part from the undercarriage suddenly drop and start scraping the road? Chances are good it was part of the exhaust system, and it's a real hazard to drive like this, so pull out the emergency kit and perform a temporary fix until you can get it to the shop.

You will need:

flashlight

old shower curtain

1 roll of mechanic's wire

1. Pull the car to a safe area and use the flashlight to determine what's dragging. If you have to lie on the ground to get a good look, spread the old shower curtain to offer some protection for your clothes.

2. Use the mechanic's wire to tie up the dragging pipe.

3. If the muffler is loose, toss it in the trunk so you won't lose it on the road.

Sometimes on a rear-wheel-drive automobile the dragging piece will be the driveshaft. Don't bother tying this one with mechanic's wire because your car won't move in this condition; head straight for the phone and call a tow truck. By the way, this problem happens when a universal joint breaks, a condition that vibrates so badly at first that if you ignore it and keep driving until the driveshaft falls off, you probably deserve to break down.

Packing for Vacation

Aside from the inevitable family squabbles, packing for vacation might not sound like the most threatening situation, but in the interest of troubleshooting, I want to give you a few tips to make your road trips safer.

 Put the heaviest weight (such as large suitcases) over the shock area so the rear of the car has less tendency to sag. If you pack too much weight at the back end of the trunk, the additional load will cause an upward tilt at the front and your headlights will shine at an odd angle. This could blind other drivers.

 Never stack baggage in a way that limits the driver's visibility. You should be able to see clearly from all windows and from your rearview mirror.

✔ Secure all items in the trunk, hatchback, or backseat. If you suffered a collision, the force of the wreck could propel loose objects forward like missiles, injuring passengers or shattering windows.

✔ And some other commonsense tips: Pack valuables out of sight; don't pack anything that might expand in the heat; carry extra garbage bags, laundry bags, and paper towels; and to avoid packing and unpacking heavy suitcases every time you stop for the night, let each passenger pack a small overnight kit that includes pajamas, one change of clothes, and toiletries.

Towing a Trailer

While we're on the subject of vacations, not every car was made for towing a trailer. Check with your repair shop about your car's capability to tow and about the weight you plan to pull.

 Install a safe, professional tow hitch on your car, and add an adapter for signal lights on the back of the trailer.

✔ Consider installing an *external transmission cooler*. Towing additional weight generates a tremendous amount of heat in the transmission, sometimes more than the transmission cooler in the radiator can dissipate. Running transmission fluid through this second cooler eliminates the risk of overheating the transmission.

✔ Be sure your car has tires rated to pull additional weight.

✔ If you've never towed a trailer before, head for a shopping center parking lot after hours to practice. Driving can be tricky, particularly backing up, even if the trailer is small.

Last But Not Least . . . Safety First

The Better Traffic Committee (BTC) places the blame for many accidents on the dangerous habits of drivers. A broken car will never cause as much damage as a selfish driver with a "me-first" attitude, and in the wrong hands a car can be just as dangerous as a gun. Review your own driving habits and practice the safety tips here:

✔ Are you a distracted, hostile driver when you're ill-tempered? Or do you find yourself too overconfident, speeding and weaving, when you're in an especially good mood? Don't let your attitude dictate your driving.

✔ Avoid driving with the window open if you're smoking a cigarette. Hot ash could get blown in your face or your lap, and your startled reaction could cause an accident.

✔ Don't eat or drink while you drive. If you're concerned with a melting ice cream cone or trying to eat a messy fast-food burger, you can bet your concentration will be diminished. Drinks, particularly hot beverages, could spill on you and not only scald you but also cause a reflex that jerks the steering wheel.

✔ Don't allow kids to jump around in the car. Insist on seat belts. Ditto for pets. Use a carrying case or a special seat belt designed to restrain enthusiastic animals.

✔ You'll constantly run into situations that require a judgment call: *Is it too foggy to drive? Can I make it another ten miles even though the gas gauge reads empty?* It's always better to err on the side of safety. The next time you face a difficult situation, think of your grandmother's lecture about how an ounce of prevention is worth a pound of cure.

✔ Don't attempt to teach another person to drive if you, yourself, are a nervous driver. First of all, I've known a lot of anxious parents who reached over and grabbed the steering wheel or tried to jam on the brakes from the passenger seat. Talk about an accident waiting to happen! Second, your hysteria could rub off and then you've got two nervous drivers in the family.

✔ Don't get overconfident just because your car has some safety features. Air bags are first on the list. They were designed to be used in conjunction with seat belts, which statistically are still the most important safety feature in the car. In combination, air bags and seat belts reduce risk of serious injury by almost 55 percent. Another thing many people don't realize is air bags deploy only if your car is involved in a frontal collision. You could be hit from the side or behind and that air bag will stay neatly tucked in its compartment. (Air bag adaptations are being developed to deploy if you're hit from the side, but not all cars have them. When purchasing your car, ask the salesperson very specific questions about the kind of air bag system it has.)

One last note about air bags and how they can *increase* risk: A recent motor club survey showed stolen air bags have surpassed theft of radio as the most common car crime. That's because a deployed air bag cannot be repacked, it must be replaced entirely. On some cars that procedure costs as much as $1,800, so car thieves have taken to stealing air bags since they bring top-dollar on the "hot" market.

Beware of Creature Comforts

One of the biggest potential hazards of twentieth-century driving is the advent of the luxury car. Automobiles these days come equipped with telephones, fax machines, drink holders, reclining seats,

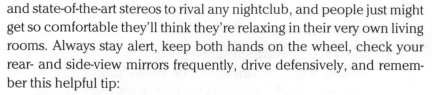
and state-of-the-art stereos to rival any nightclub, and people just might get so comfortable they'll think they're relaxing in their very own living rooms. Always stay alert, keep both hands on the wheel, check your rear- and side-view mirrors frequently, drive defensively, and remember this helpful tip:

Your living room is a stationary object.

Your car is a high-powered machine hurtling down the road at 60 mph. See the difference?

Ahh, Sweet Mysteries of Life: Recognizing Symptoms and Understanding Problems

Think back to when you were in grade school and you didn't know how to spell a word. You'd ask the teacher, who would invariably tell you to go look it up in the dictionary. Except how could you look it up if you didn't know how to spell the word in the first place? The memory of that experience has a lot to do with how I set up information in this section. I thought it would be a lot easier to list common symptoms you're likely to recognize—such as leaking fluid or a lazy engine or trouble with the steering—and then list the various problems that might be causing the symptoms.

Now that you've got some confidence and experience under your belt, I'm sure you're ready to dive right under the hood and tackle whatever problem is standing between you and the open road, but sometimes the best solution is to take your findings to the repair shop and let the pros handle it. When you do, clearly explain your car's symptoms and bring along any evidence of the problem, but be sure to give the auto technician the ultimate responsibility for diagnosing the car's condition. Many times I've heard stories about customers who walked into a shop and announced, "I need a new catalytic converter," and guess what, the shop installed a costly new catalytic converter.

Except . . . the customer got the car back and the original problem was still there since the catalytic converter wasn't the culprit after all. The customer only *thought* it was. I really think you should treat your car repair just as you would a trip to the family doctor. If you walked into a doctor's office and said, "Occasionally I have headaches so I'd like you to perform a brain transplant," and the doctor said, "Yup, you bet, one brain transplant coming up," you'd both be acting irresponsibly.

As you read this section about recognizing symptoms and understanding car problems, keep in mind that you're using the information to become a better customer, not to become the auto technician. With that clear, let's proceed.

After decades of facing customers in a repair shop, I find the best way to narrow down the list of possible problems is to rely on the five senses. When you take your car to the shop, the first questions mechanics usually ask are what does the car sound like, how does it feel, and do you see or smell anything unusual. (Okay, I admit I have never asked a customer about the sense of taste in relation to a car, so to be accurate we're only dealing with four senses here.)

Shake, Rattle, and Roll

W e're going to start with the sense of touch: how your car feels when you drive it. A perfectly performing automobile is a joy to experience, and drivers tend to take it for granted—until the first unusual shimmy or shortcoming. Then look out! All of a sudden you hate the car, and you're ready to start browsing the car lots for a replacement.

All drivers develop a *feel* for their own cars. The next time you realize something is off, wait before you worry. Take a look at the symptoms and the system in which they occur, and you can begin to plot a logical path for repairs.

Engine Won't Start

You'll experience few things more frustrating than getting into your car, all set to make an important meeting or appointment, only to discover a no-start condition in the car's engine. If you're aware of the possible causes, you may be able to fix the problem and make that meeting after all.

Basic Silly Mistake

The first reason is so simple I might insult you by suggesting it. Believe it or not, I've had customers who towed their cars to the shop because the engine wouldn't start, only to have a technician tell them that the last time they parked the car they forgot to put the transmission selector in "park." The moral here is to check the obvious stuff first.

Battery Terminals

If you turn the key to activate the starter and there's no sound at all, try your lights. If they don't work and the whole electrical system seems to be dead, then your next step is to check the battery terminals for a loose connection or for corrosion.

If the terminals are clean but loose, just tighten them. If the terminals look corroded, you can simply remove and clean them. (See Chapter 4.) Corrosion on the outside looks like whitish ash, and you'll see most of it sticking to the place where the battery terminals connect to the posts. After tightening and/or cleaning the terminals the engine should start right up.

Dead Battery

Recognizing the symptoms of a dead battery is simple. If you turn the key in the ignition and you get a groaning sound—or if it makes the usual sound but it's weaker than usual—your battery is probably low or dead. If you belong to the auto club, give it a call and the workers can jump the battery, or you could call on a friendly neighbor with a set of jumper cables. (For instructions on jumping a battery," see Chapter 6.)

But a good battery doesn't just go dead; there has to be a contributing factor and you'll find a list of possibilities.

✔ The *voltage regulator,* which controls the output of the alternator, could be restricting flow, and if that's the problem you may need more energy than the charging system is producing. On older cars the voltage regulator can be adjusted, but on newer ones it probably will have to be replaced.

✔ Some batteries require you to add water occasionally because if the level gets too low, the battery won't hold a charge. If your battery has six removable caps, check the water level.

✔ Another possibility is a malfunctioning starter demanding too much current. An engine in need of a tune-up causes the engine to crank too long trying to start and that runs down a battery too—another good argument for getting an engine tune-up before winter rolls around.

In fact, temperature can have a devastating effect on a battery. If you fully charge your battery when the temperature's 80 degrees F, it will have only 65 percent of its cranking power when the temperature drops to 32 degrees. By the time the temperature hits zero, the battery is returning only 40 percent, less than half of its cranking power. That means if your battery was only half charged to begin with, when the temperature hits zero degrees the battery will be down to just 21 percent of its cranking power.

You car needs more energy in cold weather to crank the cold engine and start it. Add to that the fact that in cold weather many cars are not driven for a long enough period to recharge the battery fully. If you go on long enough under these conditions, one day you may head out to the driveway and find the battery is too low even to start the car.

Ideally, you should put your car in the garage to protect it from winter temperatures, but if you don't have a garage, don't despair. You can still keep the car battery warm with a few tricks. You might run an extension cord out to the car and use a *small* lightbulb for extra warmth. (I've seen some customers who put large lightbulbs under the hood and ended up melting the battery!) Some people put blankets over the car's hood in really cold weather, and that's okay too. If you live in an area with really frigid weather, I suggest you buy a small battery charger. It's called a *trickle charger* because it charges just a few amps per hour, but that's still enough keep the battery warm so it has full cranking capacity when you want to start the car. Trickle chargers, which run about $25 to $50, are available in auto parts stores.

Choke Butterfly

As we discovered in our lesson on dead batteries, sometimes you have to look *outside* of the car to help determine the problem. Cold weather can also affect the choke butterfly on your carburetor, making it stick open. Of course, this is a possibility only if your car has a carburetor; if you have a fuel-injection system, this doesn't apply.

If the choke butterfly is stuck, the engine cranks fast and sounds normal, but still, the engine won't start. No need to panic over this one: All you have to do to solve the problem is open the hood, remove the lid from the air cleaner so you can reach the choke butterfly, and pop it shut.

To help prevent a recurrence, make a trip to your local auto parts store and buy an aerosol can of carburetor cleaner. Spray the carburetor cleaner around the choke, work it back and forth a few times, and you won't have to face this problem the next time temperatures drop.

But choke butterflies can also stick *shut*. It's a common problem in cars built before the 1980s, and it causes a different reaction entirely. If the choke butterfly is closed, the engine will start easily and run fine, but only for a few minutes. If it doesn't open as the engine warms up, it causes a flooding condition, the car will stall, and absolutely no amount of cranking can get it to restart. Then you'll have to open the hood, pull off the air cleaner lid to give you access to the choke butterfly, and flip it open. *Voilá,* your car will start. Prevent a repeat of this problem by cleaning the choke area with a few sprays from an aerosol can of carburetor cleaner.

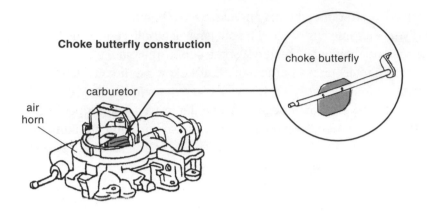

Choke butterfly construction

choke butterfly

carburetor

air
horn

Starter and Flywheel

Sometimes the engine won't start, but your car makes a tremendous racket in its effort. And when I say "tremendous racket," I'm talking about the kind of screeching, scraping sound you might hear from an alley cat looking for a little romance. It may be intermittent at first, then gradually become more frequent as the condition worsens. You could have a bad starter or the teeth could be stripped off the flywheel, and either one of these conditions goes beyond basic do-it-yourself repair. Call the tow truck and leave this one for the pros.

Flooded Engine

When the engine is flooded, the starter keeps turning the crankshaft but the car won't start, and you'll also smell a strong odor of gasoline. Instead of gas vapor, liquid gasoline has gotten to the spark plugs and has literally soaked them. For instructions on handling a flooded engine, see Chapter 6.

If none of these problems sounds like what's happening in your car and the engine still won't start, you might be the victim of a miscellaneous electronic or computer problem. Sorry, folks, but these fall under the Don't Try This at Home heading, so get the car to a repair shop for a diagnosis by the experts.

Engine That Misses

We say an engine is "missing" when one or more cylinders fails to take its turn in turning the crankshaft. The result is a skip and loss of smoothness as the engine runs, something akin to riding a bucking bronco every time you step on the gas. When it's idling it may feel rough, even rough enough to shake the car.

An engine miss might be caused by a bad spark plug or wire. It could be a fuel-injection problem, a computer problem, or one of several more serious engine problems. This condition is a definite candidate for a trip to the shop. Even though you could continue to drive it, with an engine miss your vehicle is wasting gasoline and creating more pollution.

There is one case of a rough idle that you might want to check out yourself: when the rough, shaky idle is accompanied by a hissing from under the hood. A vacuum hose may have popped off, and if you can locate it by sound, repairing it is simply a matter of reconnecting the hose.

Lazy, Powerless Engine

I always describe a lazy, powerless vehicle as a gutless car that has trouble getting out of its own way. And if you like high performance in an engine as much as I do, you know a car with a lazy engine is a royal pain on the road.

Engines become lazy for lots of different reasons. Your best bet is to take the car to a skilled shop with a good engine analyzer. To give you an idea of just how advanced a machine an engine analyzer is, if there were such a thing as a "people analyzer," you could connect a couple of wires to a person and immediately know the pulse rate, blood pressure, heart performance, temperature, bone density, muscle, and tendon conditions and so on. All that from just one machine.

By connecting an engine analyzer to the engine, a technician can determine very quickly just where the problem lies because it gives a reading of everything happening in the engine. This piece of equipment

"You say to-ma-to, I say tune-up..."

Several times now I've used the terms "tune-up" and "performance check," and I want to stress that those two terms are not interchangeable. "Tune-up" is on its way out because it only refers to a procedure for early-model cars. In the old days, a tune-up was a must twice a year. It included replacing points, the condenser, the rotor and spark plugs, and the air and fuel filters. Ignition timing and the carburetor both received adjustments, and the grand total came to around fifty bucks.

With today's engines, computers control the adjustments. There are no more points and condensers to install, and cars have so many computer-operated parts that the auto repair industry now uses the term "engine performance check" when it's referring to later-model vehicles. Have one done annually. The technician should replace spark plugs, check or replace wires, clean or replace the air and fuel filters, and run an engine analyzer to detect other problems. The cost of an engine performance check falls between $50 to $150, depending on what other part replacements are indicated. The key to a good engine performance check is to have it done at a shop where techs have both the equipment and the knowledge to handle it.

costs between $25,000 to $35,000 and the technician must be skilled to interpret it, so don't be shy about asking the repair shop manager about his or her training. The good news is a simple tune-up or engine performance check might be all that's required to restore the car to health.

Don't be alarmed if you aren't the kind of driver who really revels in engine performance and think you won't be able to tell the difference between a good engine and a lazy one. Most later-model cars come equipped with an indicator on the dash that will light up and tell you to "check engine." Auto technicians are able to check the engine with a monitor or a computer card that points to the problem area, but a few clues can help you figure out one pretty obvious cause, and that's if the car seems to be suffering from some kind of exhaust restriction. The catalytic converter, which is part of your emissions system, will cause a car to lose power if it becomes plugged up. Chemical compounds that aid in the emissions process exist in the form of pellets or a honeycomb. A poorly running engine or overly rich fuel mixture can cause these pellets to fuse together in a solid mass, or plug the honeycomb, both of which restrict the flow of exhaust gases.

If the catalytic converter is the cause of your lazy engine, then the car will actually go slower the more you accelerate and move better when you accelerate lightly. The best preventive measure is to maintain your engine well, because this condition requires a trip to the repair shop where the catalytic converter will be replaced at an average cost of $150 to $200.

Lazy Car Due to Transmission Problems

Some problems develop in the transmission. This is a tough break because they make a car feel lazy, but they aren't easy to pin down as transmission-related. However, we all get used to the "feel" of our cars, so you just might be able to detect the source of the problem from a couple of symptoms I'll list here.

Complete Loss of Power from a Dead Stop

The part connecting the transmission to the engine, the *torque converter,* is active on take-off only, where it multiplies power internally. If it malfunctions, you'll notice the loss of power only when you try to move the car from a dead stop. In fact, you can put the gas pedal all the way to the floor and the car will still barely creep. If your car is lazy only on take-off but feels normal once you're moving, the torque converter is one likely possibility.

High Gear Start

Another possibility in the transmission is a stuck valve in the governor, which will prevent the transmission from dropping back to low gear when the car comes to a stop. That means it will still be in high gear when you try to move the car again, resulting in a real feeling of laziness. Often metallic particles wearing from some area in the transmission are to blame for the sticking governor valve, a condition that usually indicates the start of a more serious problem. Get the car to the repair shop to prevent more expensive repairs down the line.

Stalling Engine

Most everyone has experienced a frustrating stall at some point, and in the old days to fix it you'd just turn a screw on the carburetor. Not the case these days because the sophistication of newer-model cars means a stall could originate in the fuel system or electrical system, and in certain cars it might even be a transmission problem. If your car stalls only on infrequent and isolated occasions, I'd ignore it. Ditto if it only happens when the weather gets really cold. After all, are you at your best when it's freezing outside? I know I'm not.

Frequent stalling can be more than an annoyance; it's got the potential to be dangerous too. If the car stalls during a turn, you're stuck without power steering or power brakes, and repeated stalling is hard on the starter if you keep cranking over and over again. If this is happening to you, I'd say once you get your car started, drive straight to the repair shop. The auto technician will look for the problem using that great diagnostic tool I told you about, the engine analyzer. Since stalling is caused by either the fuel or electronic systems, repair costs will vary depending on where the problem originated.

Stalling engines due to automatic transmission problems are another story entirely. In fact, they're a pretty recent phenomenon. Some automatic transmissions were designed to improve fuel economy with the addition of a clutch disc inside the torque converter that locks up in high gear. A malfunction can cause the clutch to stay locked on even when the car comes to a stop, causing the engine to stall. Here's where you get stuck in a kind of vicious circle. Your car continues to stall every time you put it into gear, then it cools down and it's fine, and then as you drive it gets hot again and stalls until you let it cool down. The good news is the repair for this does not require taking the transmission out of the car, so your auto technician can fix the problem for a little more than $100. (If they have to take out the transmission, the repair price goes up by several hundred dollars.)

If your car has an automatic transmission and you're getting all worked up anticipating this problem, you can relax because not all automatic transmissions have this feature, and not all of those that do are prone to develop a problem. If you have a stalling problem, ask the technician if the transmission could be causing it. Too many times a car with this condition is misdiagnosed, and it comes into the shop after a whole lot of money has been spent on other parts in an attempt to fix it.

Transmission Performance Problems

Most people dread a malfunction in the automatic transmission because it has a reputation for being expensive to repair. Admittedly, that reputation is often well deserved. But not all automatic transmission problems are serious, and early attention can cut costs.

Loss of a Gear

If you're missing a gear, then your car will either not have all its forward gears or it won't move backward; either way there's nothing you can do except take it to the repair shop. If you lose reverse, but everything feels fine moving forward, then it's okay to drive the car to the repair shop. If you lose forward, you'll have to go with the tow truck—although I actually once had a customer who drove to the shop in reverse *for miles* just to avoid paying for the tow. It was an interesting stunt, but I don't recommend it.

No Movement

If your car won't move in either direction, the first thing you should do is check to make sure your parking brake is released. If the brake is released and your car still won't move in either direction, check the transmission fluid level. (See Chapter 5.) Automobile transmissions are hydraulically operated, and if the car's not moving, the fluid level may be too low.

Adding transmission fluid is an easy repair, and if it was the cause of the problem, your car will certainly move again. But after you add the fluid you'll want to investigate why it disappeared in the first place. Either drive or tow the car to the shop and let the professionals diagnose the true guilty party.

Slipping

Have you ever stepped on the accelerator and found the engine raced but the car itself wouldn't move? It happens in manual transmissions because the clutch is slipping. In an automatic transmission, a low fluid level could be to blame, or it could have an internal problem causing a slip in any gear or on any shift.

Transmissions are far too tricky for do-it-yourselfers, so take the car to a transmission shop. The technicians will determine what's wrong by road-testing the car and then dropping the transmission pan for an internal inspection. They may use a monitor to check electronic controls on later-model cars or use a gauge to check internal pressure. Any information you can give the technician is helpful. How often does it happen? Is it only a cold or hot problem? Does it only happen on a hill or when you accelerate quickly to pass? Go to the shop armed with information and you could cut down on the time it takes the tech to diagnose the problem—and that means a lower bill for you.

No Upshift

When a transmission won't shift into high gear, we say it has no upshift. It feels as if you can't get any speed no matter how hard you step on the gas. Once again, let the transmission expert find the cause. The good news is the loss of an upshift can be a very minor problem, caused by something simple, such as a bad vacuum hose, a bad cable, or even a bad electrical switch. On a few occasions the cause is more serious, so keep your fingers crossed while you're waiting for the technician to come back with a final diagnosis.

By the way, unless you live very close to the repair shop, you should have the vehicle towed. Driving long distances in low gear can cause engine overheating.

Won't Come Out of Park

This is one of those really maddening problems because no matter how hard you pull, jiggle, jerk, or swear, you just can't move the lever out of "park." Fords of the 1970s and '80s had this problem. Today we see it happening mostly with Chrysler front-wheel-drive vehicles—but be aware that on some later-model cars you cannot move the lever out of "park" unless your foot is on the brake. If you're experiencing this problem in an unfamiliar car, step on the brake as you pull the lever, and see if that does the trick. If you're parked on a hill and didn't use your parking brake, then go make your phone call for help. Under these conditions if you keep trying to force the lever, you'll only succeed in damaging the linkage or cable.

Now, some of you might be thinking *This would have been a good tip to know* before *I forced the lever and damaged the linkage or cable.* If you're one of the people who has already gone too far, then get it fixed and develop the following habit. If you follow this routine faithfully, you'll never get stuck in park again.

When stopping the car:

1. Stop the car with your foot on the brake, but keep the engine running.

2. Put on the parking brake.

3. *Then* put the transmission lever in "park."

4. Turn off the engine.

When restarting the car:

1. Start the car, leaving your foot on the brake.

2. Move the transmission lever out of "park."

3. *Then* release the parking brake.

By applying the brake first, you prevent the *parking pawl* (a little hook that must catch on a gear in order to hold the car) from positioning too deep. If the car drifts even a few inches as you put it in park, the parking pawl will be very tight against the gear and all of the weight of the automobile will be against it. You prevent that from happening when you apply the parking brake first.

Steering Problems

Steering should be effortless, so if the time comes when you notice that turning takes more effort than usual, explore the problem.

Loss of Power Steering Fluid

If your car has power steering and you not only have trouble turning the wheel but also hear a growling sound when you turn, then you've run low on power steering fluid. Add more power steering fluid (see Chapter 4) and it should feel just fine, but as always, you'll still want to drop by the repair shop to locate the source of the fluid leak.

Car Out of Alignment

Front-end alignment is the geometric setting of the front wheels to provide easier steering and optimum tire wear, so if your car's front end is out of alignment, then it may be difficult to steer. It's easy enough to tell if the alignment is the culprit here. Just take a look at your tires and see if they appear scuffed on the outside edges. A bad toe-in adjustment results in front tires that tend to drag on turns so the rubber will look as if it were dragged across the pavement. Take your car to a repair shop that offers alignment services and have the problem checked out.

Alignment vs. Balance

Front-end alignment and wheel balance are two completely different procedures; still, consumers frequently use the two terms interchangeably. We've already covered the definition of alignment, so let's now get the story straight on tire balance. Did you ever drive a car on the highway and cruise smoothly until you hit 60 mph and suddenly the car has the shakes so badly you can feel it all the way up to the steering wheel? If you sped up it smoothed out, and if you slowed down it was okay too, but around 60 mph you were rockin' and rollin'. Chances are one of your tires was out of balance.

Tires have so much rubber molded on them that it is impossible to keep them completely true. Even one or two ounces of weight on any part of the tire can pose a problem at higher speeds. As the tire spins on its axis (the axle), the centrifugal force created by the speed of the wheel will cause the extra weight to hit the pavement on each rotation and cause a shimmy. The weight of the imbalance and its position determine the speed at which the shimmy will occur.

If you mistake this for an alignment problem you could pay for the alignment, get out on the highway, and find your car still suffers from the shimmy! To repair a balance problem properly, your tire technician will perform a *wheel balance* by strategically adding lead weights to the wheel to counteract the extra weight.

The only way wheel alignment and tire balance ever affect each other is when a car that is out of alignment causes uneven tire wear. The worn tire would then develop the additional problem of tire imbalance.

Rack and Pinion Steering

Your steering problem may be from an internal fault in the rack and pinion component, a newer type of steering system that replaces the old-style gear box. Rack and pinion steering is lighter, more compact, and has fewer moving parts. If you can hardly turn the steering wheel when the car is cold (cold because it's been sitting overnight, not cold because of the weather), but then it does fine after a few turns, suspect a problem in the rack and pinion steering. An auto technician will have to repair this, but I suggest you check with your dealership first to see if this problem is covered under factory warranty. (On some GM cars, it was extended past the normal warranty.)

Pulls to One Side When Car Is Not Braking

The first thing to do in this case is check the air pressure on your front tires, because a car will pull toward the side where the tire is low. Don't depend on judging a tire by sight, though, because it's almost impossible to be accurate. Get out your handy tire gauge and check the pressure. If you detect a low tire, fill it with air at the service station. The pull should disappear, but remember to let a pro check the tire to find the leak.

But what happens if you check the tire pressure and it turns out to be fine, but your car still pulls to one side? One of the most likely causes of a pull then would be the caster adjustment, which is probably out in the front-end alignment. (Caster adjustment controls a straight-ahead steer.) A lot of times my customers won't consider this to be the problem because they say they recently had the front end aligned. Remember, you can knock a front end out of alignment with something as simple as hitting a curb, so don't eliminate this as a potential cause for steering that pulls, just because you had a recent alignment.

Suspension Problems

Does your car have a mind of its own when you go around curves? Does it sway on turns or feel wild on winding roads? Or maybe the car hits a bump and just continues to bounce? In cases like this, blame bad shocks or struts. They may even cause the front end of the car to take a dive when you brake hard or to bottom out frequently on hills.

Testing shocks and struts is a simple procedure. Stand in front of the car and, with both hands on the hood, push the car down as hard as you can. If the car bounces once and returns to place your shocks or struts are in okay shape. But if the car continues to bounce up and down a few times, you need to have the shocks or struts checked by a professional. The lifetime of shocks and struts vary, but it's not unusual to need a replacement at 24,000 miles. Severe service such as driving over rough roads and potholes frequently shortens the lifespan of shocks and struts.

Brake Performance Problems

Brake problems aren't just a simple matter of irritation or inconvenience. A problem in the brakes has the potential to be life-threatening, so make sure repairs in this area take top priority.

Soft Spongy Pedal

If you step on the brake pedal and it feels so soft and mushy that you have to pump it to get the car to stop, you might have a problem in the hydraulic brake system—such as a low fluid level. Since leaking brake fluid indicates a developing problem in the master or the wheel cylinders, you'll definitely want to have an expert check this out.

I've known people who have driven cars with spongy brakes for a long time, but frankly, I think that's foolish. You might be able to get away with it if you're a very cautious, careful driver, but sooner or later you'll come across that emergency situation when you don't have time to baby a spongy brake—and that could be deadly.

Remember, *stopping* the car is infinitely more important than *starting* it, so this isn't the time to be a frugal. Spend the money to have an expert check your brakes.

Inability to Stop

This is every driver's nightmare. The most likely cause would be the total loss of brake fluid, but thankfully today's brake systems have such safe designs the chances of a total brake failure are slim. (Just in case you're worried you might defy the odds, see Chapter 6 for complete instructions.) If you experience a problem stopping, don't try to drive the car again, not even to the repair shop. Call a tow truck and let the professionals fix the brakes before you take the car back on the road.

Hard Pedal That Resists Stopping

If you practically have to stand on your brake pedal to get the car to stop, you might be facing a malfunction in your power brake unit. If you're game (and why not at least give it a try, right?), you can lift up the hood while the engine is running and listen for a vacuum leak. It would sound like a hissing near the power brake unit, which is a large round unit mounted directly behind the brake master cylinder right in front of the firewall. If you can trace the hissing sound to a hose that became disconnected, just secure the hose back in place. If you can't locate a disconnected hose, then you're off to a repair shop.

There's another instance when you might experience the hard pedal that won't stop the car: when your brake lining is worn low or the brakes are out of adjustment. Once again, this is repair shop time, and the rule is: *Never delay the trip to the repair shop when it involves your brakes.*

Parking Brake Doesn't Work

If your parking brake doesn't hold your car, then park very carefully and, of course, be sure the transmission is in the "park" position (or in first gear, if your car has a manual transmission). The root of this problem could be parking brake cables that are out of adjustment, or a broken mechanism that actually applies the brakes. But the most common cause for parking brake failure is the seizing of the cables because of rust and lack of use.

This problem warrants a trip to the shop, although it's one you might have been able to avoid in the first place. You can prevent seizing caused by dryness by using the parking brake on a regular basis, regardless of whether you park on a flat surface or on a hill. Adopt this habit and you'll cross at least one problem off your list of worries.

Trust your sense of touch. If something doesn't feel right to you, then it probably isn't. After all, you're the one who has to drive the car every day. My recommendation is get to know your vehicle well, because every car feels a little different, handles a particular way, has one or two idiosyncracies to make it unique. Once you develop a personal relationship with your car, you'll be able to spot a performance problem before the car even reaches the end of your block. Believe me, this kind of knowledge buys a lot of self-confidence behind the wheel.

Use Your Common Scents

A malfunctioning automobile sends out some very distinctive smells to lead you to the source of your problem, so don't be embarrassed to sniff around—literally—for clues.

Gasoline

If you smell gasoline (and I don't mean just an occasional whiff after you fill the tank, I mean you *really* smell gasoline), immediately look for the source. In most circumstances, the gasoline odor is coming from a leak, and just about anything in the fuel system has the potential to be responsible.

If the fuel tank, fuel lines, or fuel pump leak, the proof usually will be beneath the car, so check there first. Look for a puddle or something dripping. Dip your finger in the puddle and give it a sniff. You'll recognize the smell of gasoline.

If you don't see any evidence of a leak beneath your car, then move on to the next likely suspect: the carburetor or fuel-injection system. A problem here will spill fuel out onto the top of the engine. Sometimes you'll be able to see a leak, but if it's under something that keeps it from being visible, you're out of luck. In some cases, the smell isn't coming from a leak but from a flooded engine.

Gasoline leaks have the potential to be dangerous, so have your technician check them out. *Do not* drive the car if gasoline is leaking profusely over the top of the engine, because then there's a danger of a fire, but if the gas leak is minor and if it's only a short distance to the shop, there should be no problem in driving the car there yourself.

I have one final but very important point about gasoline leaks: *Never* park your car in the garage if you smell gasoline. As gasoline evaporates, it leaves a vapor buildup that gets heavy in the garage (the odor could even seep into your house), and the garage vapors create potential for an explosion if exposed to a spark, even from something as small as a light switch. Better to leave the car in the driveway that night and get it to the repair shop first thing in the morning.

Hot, Burning Oil Odor

Sometimes a car just smells "hot," and chances are the smell is coming from oil leaking onto a hot exhaust pipe. The oil is literally just burning there the same way oil burns and smells in a frying pan, but unless the leak in your car is severe you probably won't notice any smoke.

Oil isn't the only fluid that can leak onto the exhaust system. Transmission fluid and power steering fluid can leak there too, but unless you have equipment to jack up the car, you may not be able to determine what's happening.

You may be able to identify the problem if a lot of smoke is billowing from beneath the car, or if you have to add engine oil or a fluid frequently, but an automotive technician will have to fix the problem. The engine, transmission, and power steering all have a number of different places that might leak.

"Burnt Toast" Smell

Smoldering wires emit a nasty acrid smell like badly burned toast. People aren't aware of how many thousands of feet of wire snake through a car, and a short in any one of them will cause a little smoldering. Your auto technician can determine the source of the problem, but if the odor is very strong and lingers after the engine is turned off, have the tech come to you or have the car towed. Until that help arrives, disconnect the battery terminal so the source of the electricity is off and the problem in the wire can't cause further damage.

"Rotten Egg" Odor

As long as we're talking about food smells, I'll mention the "rotten egg" odor next. If your car is giving off this awful smell, which is similar to sulfur, it indicates a problem in the catalytic converter, which is a part of the emissions control located in the exhaust system. You may have a problem with how the car is burning fuel, and if you continue to drive with this condition, your catalytic converter will clog up. Believe me, this is a hefty repair.

Sweet, Steamy Smell

If you get a sweet, steamy odor after the car is thoroughly warmed up, chances are good it's leaking hot coolant, which is a mixture of water and antifreeze. If the leak is very bad, you'll probably even notice steam under the hood. You may want to try to locate the source of the leak yourself, but since you'll notice the smell only when the engine is hot, be extremely careful as you investigate.

A leak can occur at the radiator, any of the hoses, or the water pump. If you're very handy or if you're feeling adventurous, just replace the leaking hose yourself. Of course, you'll want to wait until the car has cooled down before you do it. If you don't repair the problem, the coolant will continue to leak until it's lost so much fluid that the car overheats.

Another reason for a sweet, steamy smell is a leaking heater core. Can you see a leak on the floor of your car under the dash? If so, take it to the repair shop and point it out to your auto technician.

Brake Odor

I can describe the odor from overheating brakes in one word: horrible. You're most likely to notice the smell after you've parked the car and you're exiting it, so sniff around to see if you can tell from which wheel, or wheels, the smell is coming. If you can pin down the source of the smell, then *carefully* touch the wheel to see if it's hot.

A problem in the hydraulic application of the brakes could allow the friction material to drag. On disc brakes, the caliper that applies the disc pad may be sticking. On drum brakes, the sticking part could be the wheel cylinder that applies the brake shoes. In both cases the brake lining is dragging and overheating.

Brake problems sound serious, but there are a couple of harmless causes for the brake odor that you'll want to check out before you take the car to the shop:

✔ You might detect a faint odor if you've just had new brakes put on the car, but it should disappear after a day or two.

✔ You also might smell brake odor if you've been in very heavy traffic, especially downhill traffic, and you've been using your brakes extensively. They may be hot enough to smell at the time, but they'll be okay once they have a chance to cool down.

In any other case, you should play it safe. If the brake smell is a continuing problem, head for the repair shop.

Burning Rubber

You've heard people talk about "burning rubber," and the expression really means skidding your tires very hard. Occasionally we all skid, but

Give Your Brakes a Break

Severely overheated brakes don't just smell, they don't perform well either. If you come down a long hill with the brake pedal partially depressed the whole time, the brake lining will get overheated and affect your ability to stop the car. Be kinder to your brakes when you're descending a hill by using your transmission. Pump the brakes lightly to slow the car, then move your transmission selector lever to second on a steep hill until you've slowed down, then move into first.

Both automatic and standard transmissions can serve in this way, so use them. Many motorists avoid using their transmissions for fear of provoking costly repairs, but it really won't hurt the transmission and it's a safer way to take the hill.

you won't get much of an odor unless you're spinning the tire to the point that it almost smokes, and then the smell is horrible. Your basic careful driver probably won't face the smell of burning rubber—but if you drive like a cowboy, jam on the brakes, and skid to a stop, not only is the odor bad but you're also wasting money and doing damage to your car. That black streak left on the road after a hard skid is actually tread off your tire. The solution here is to practice a little behavior modification.

Musty, Damp Smell

If the inside of your car is starting to smell like the damp, musty basement in your great aunt Millie's house, it's probably because moisture is getting into your upholstery or carpeting. Any leak around window moldings or inside the trunk will dampen carpeting, and, if it's an area

Dangerous, Deadly... and Difficult to Detect

One very dangerous gas that does not leave an odor is *carbon monoxide,* which is emitted in the exhaust of an automobile. In addition to being odorless it is also colorless, and, because the side effects of too much carbon monoxide come on gradually, a person can be overcome before even realizing there's a problem.

You and everyone in your family should know the symptoms of carbon monoxide poisoning. As you breathe in carbon monoxide, even small amounts, the blood cells latch onto it instead of oxygen. You may feel lethargic at first, then drowsy. Skin takes on a reddish appearance, your ears may ring, and you'll experience some nausea. In its final stages the poison will render a person unconscious and eventually prove fatal.

Never sit for long periods of time in a closed car with the engine running, something people tend to do in winter to take advantage of the heater. Avoid this hazard by dressing warmly in winter, even packing a few blankets in your car—a much safer way to keep warm while you're parked.

If you know that you're driving a car with a bad exhaust system, drive with the windows open, and if you think you're experiencing any of the symptoms of carbon monoxide poisoning, immediately get lots of fresh air, then follow up by a trip to the hospital.

that's difficult to dry out, the dampness will breed mold and mildew. Once you identify the cause of the smell, dry out the damp area thoroughly by leaving open the windows or trunk lid, ideally on a sunny day. For severe moisture problems use an electric fan. After it's dried, use a deodorant spray designed for a car's interior.

Broken Window Seals

If old, crumbling weather strips or window moldings are allowing moisture into your car, you can purchase tubes of special black silicon for sealing windshield and window leaks. Just apply it the same way you seal the edges of your bathtub with a tube of caulk. It's just as hard to do a neat job with the window sealant as it is with the bathroom caulk, though, so if you'd rather not mess with this, take the car to your auto repair shop.

One way to ward off the problem in the first place is to avoid parking in hot, direct sunlight. Long-term sun and heat exposure cause the rubber molding to dry and crack, and that leads to leaks. Choose a garage or park in a shady area whenever possible.

Leaking Heater Core

A leaky heater core could cause a damp, musty smell too. Leaking coolant wets the carpet on the floor under the dash, and again, the result is mold and mildew. One way to tell if the heater core is to blame is if your windows steam up whenever the engine is running. After you replace the heater core, dry out and clean the carpeting.

Careless Habits

Another simple reason for damp carpets and upholstery is simple carelessness. If you frequently leave your car windows open, you increase the chances of seats getting soaked during a rain or of condensation forming inside the car. One good rainstorm can soak upholstery deeply enough that it just can't dry out, and before you know it you're facing that awful moldy odor.

· · ·

Heater core construction and location

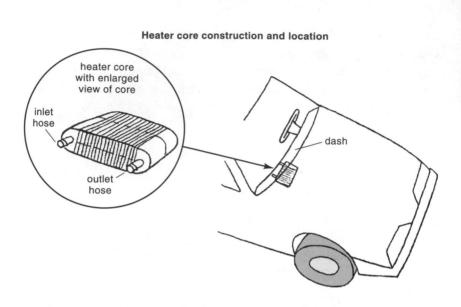

heater core
with enlarged
view of core

inlet
hose

outlet
hose

dash

Your sense of smell is very helpful—and actually serves as a safety aid—when it comes to detecting car problems. Pay attention to odors the same way you would a noise or a performance problem.

Smoke Gets in Your Eyes

Get familiar with what your car's normal components look like, and you'll be able to identify many problems with a knowledgeable glance. Take a few minutes to lift up the hood and understand the stuff that's under there. (It's okay to use the car's manual as a map; this isn't a quiz.) You have to do this on your own car, though, because cars are all very different mechanically, and it doesn't help you to learn on any model other than the one you'll be maintaining.

If you find yourself staring at your car for an extended period of time and still don't know a fan belt from a seat belt, move to Plan B: Drive the car to your favorite auto technician armed with a list of questions and a box of doughnuts. Ask the tech to point out the parts of your car, front to back, top to bottom, even get the car up on a lift so you can see underneath. It's worth the trip (and the doughnuts) to get a really good look, and most mechanics I know love to teach.

The following pages detail the most common problems you can detect by sight, along with some suggestions for solving them.

Tires

Quality radial tires have a potential lifetime of at least 40,000 miles. Proper inflation, good front-end alignment, and routine rotation all help. Screeching stops from high speeds and squealing high-speed turns rob tires of many miles, and you drifters who hit curbs and scrape sidewalls have to know the tires are taking the brunt of your bad behavior.

Problems with the tires are probably the easiest to identify by sight because tires never lie. *Where* the tires are worn will tell exactly *how* the tires got that way so you can prevent a recurrence.

Even Tire Wear

If the tire is suffering signs of regular use, you'll see even tread wear, but you will also see smooth bare strips running horizontally. These are wear bars that are built into the tread to tell you when it's time for new tires.

**Tire with even tread wear and
exposed tread bars**

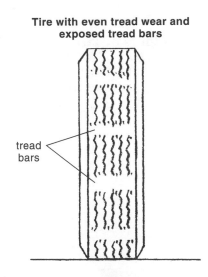

tread
bars

Worn Tread in Center of Tire

If the tire has tread on the outside but it's smooth down the center, the problem is overinflation. Too much air in the tire causes the center to bulge out, and the center of the tire will wear out faster than the outside.

Center tread wear

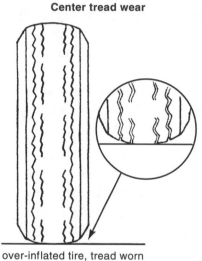

over-inflated tire, tread worn
in center, good tread on sides

Worn Tread on Outside of Tire

If the tire has tread down the center but it's worn on the outsides, you've been driving on a tire that's underinflated. The center buckles in, and the wear takes place on the outside edges.

Outside tread wear

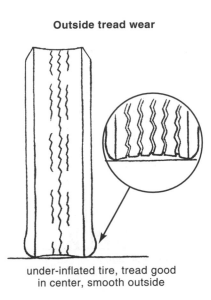

under-inflated tire, tread good
in center, smooth outside

Half Tread, Half Worn

If your tire has good tread on one side and is worn smooth on the other, this indicates a problem with the camber adjustment. After you replace the tire, schedule a trip to the shop for a front-end alignment.

Side tread wear

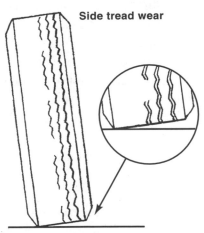

bad camber adjustment/alignment out:
worn tread one side, good tread on side

Abnormal wear

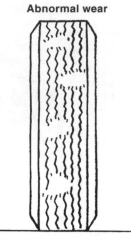

tire with abnormal cupping

Abnormal, Uneven Tire Wear

Bad shock absorbers or struts will cause abnormal wear or cups in the tread of a tire.

Since tire wear is sometimes just a symptom of another problem, don't think you're done once you've replaced the bad tire. Over- or underinflation is an owner problem you can take care of, but if the way the tire wore tells you to get a front-end alignment or replace shocks and struts, then schedule the appointment. Otherwise those brand-new tires you put on the car are going to wear down in exactly the same way as the last set, and you've just wasted a lot of money.

One important thing about tires: Never replace just one. Replace both front tires together and both back tires together. If you can afford it, replace all four at the same time. And to get the most value out of your tires, be sure to rotate them on a regular schedule. (See Chapter 5.)

Belts and Hoses

If you've spent some time studying what's under the hood, you know it takes several belts and hoses to keep your car running. Belts and hoses develop some problems on a gradual basis, so you'll be able to see cracks and crevices long before the parts break completely and you're left stranded on the side of the road.

Sometimes cracks on a hose are caused by clamps cutting into the rubber. If it's cut, you have no choice but to replace the hose. On belts, newer designs don't show wear as readily, so pay attention to the change schedule listed in your owner's manual. Other belts show signs of deteriorating that you can see most clearly on the smooth back side of the belt. Some cars offer little diagrams of how to change a belt, but I think the adjustment on a task like this is critical, so unless you're familiar with this repair, leave it for the professionals. Simple replacement costs under $25, although serpentine belts require a more labor-intensive installation, so that can go as high as $90.

The same holds true for worn radiator and heater hoses. When a hose is old, cracked, or the rubber has hardened, or if it feels soft and squishy, let a technician replace it. Costs will run from $20 to as high as $40. In the interest of preventive medicine, I recommend replacing all of the hoses at the same time even if not all of them appear to be damaged.

Battery Terminals

Look over the battery terminals. A buildup of corrosion is the forerunner to problems, especially on late-model, electronically controlled cars. On these, the slightest electrical malfunction can cause big problems; in fact, some dirty terminals will cause the car to go into "limp mode," where the transmission won't shift and the car must limp into the shop for repairs. Avoid this by performing routine maintenance on your battery. (See Chapter 4.)

Suspension

Stand a short distance away from your car and take a good look at it from both the front and the back. If the car appears to be sagging lower on one side, it indicates a problem in the suspension. You may have weak or broken springs or a bad strut.

Undercarriage

"Undercarriage" refers to all of the parts on the underside of your car that you would see if you were lying under it or looking at it when it was up on a lift. Chemicals and the salt used for ice and snow removal collect on the undercarriage can cause rust, even if these parts have corrosion protection. Use clean water to spray the underbody, paying particular attention to the fuel lines, frame, and exhaust system. If necessary loosen any caked-on mud or debris before you spray.

Shocks and Struts

Dents on the body of either a shock or strut, or torn or missing protective boots, indicate damage that can lead to leaks. You'll spot the leak from shocks and struts easily because it runs down the housing and road dirt sticks to it.

Worn CV Boots on Front-Wheel-Drive Vehicles

You can easily sight a problem with a boot on the constant velocity joint. The next time you park your front-wheel-drive vehicle, turn the wheels outward so you can see the CV boot, which looks like a little rubber accordion attached to the back of the wheel. These boots are the only means of retaining lubrication on the CV joints. Without that lubrication, CV joints can wear and fail, amounting to some pretty expensive repairs.

Axle boot or CV joint replacement requires professional attention. See your auto technician for repairs.

Blurry Windshield When Using Wipers

If you can't see any better with the windshield wipers than you could without them, investigate the wiper blades. In some cases a twig or leaf is caught under the blade and that's what's causing the smear. If the problem seems to be from worn-out blades, then head down to the local auto parts store and buy a new pair.

Follow the directions on the box and you'll see replacing windshield wipers is a matter of popping and snapping a couple of pieces together—no tougher than your average toy Erector set. Some blades require a screwdriver to loosen a release clip before the assembly comes apart. It's a good idea to replace the entire blade at once, since the springs lose their tension over time, but there are occasions when only the rubber is damaged and the rest of the wiper is intact. The rubber is a separate part of the blade assembly, so you can change it easily by snapping it out.

If you live in a climate where winter weather and ice do a real job on the wiper blades, look for a set of winter-weather blades. They're thicker and sturdier than the regular blades to resist caking up with ice and snow, and in the snowy climate where I live I find them to be a real life-saver.

Exhaust System

The only part of the exhaust system you can see is the end of the tailpipe that sticks out from under the rear of the car. Extensive rust on this part is easy to spot. To get a really good look at the exhaust system you'd have to get under the car, and to do that safely you need a floor jack and jack stands. If you don't have these, take the car to your favorite repair shop and ask them to put the car on a lift. Hangers, clamps, and the pipes themselves will all show visible deterioration.

Exhaust systems now last much longer than on early-model cars, because the metal is treated to prevent rust. Lifetimes, however, do vary, not only due to climate and salt or dirt but also because of engine conditions. Poorly running engines can cause the pipes to deteriorate on the inside, and this is more of a problem nowadays than external rust. The cowboy driver who scrapes the undercarriage of the car also contributes to a shorter life for the exhaust system.

Smoke

In old Western movies, Indians sent out messages by smoke signals. Well, every now and then your car does the same thing, and if you know how to read them, you'll have no trouble correcting the problem.

Blue-gray Smoke

If your car's tailpipe is billowing blue-gray smoke, then you know engine oil is burning with the fuel. Years ago that meant a very serious engine problem, usually worn rings on the pistons. That can still happen today, but thanks to the improved quality of the parts, it's not as frequent a cause. Now the most common causes are clogged oil passages and bad valve stem seals. You can prevent the clogged passages by changing the engine oil regularly.

If you see a little blue-gray smoke when you first start up the car in the morning but it clears up as you continue to drive the car, don't do anything (except swear that you'll change the oil regularly from now on). But if your engine uses lots of oil and you see the blue-gray smoke as long as the engine is running, then the car needs help—the professional kind.

Coal-black Smoke

Black smoke from the tailpipe means your car is getting too rich of a fuel mixture. On a cold morning, at startup you'll see black smoke for a minute or two because the fuel system has adjusted a richer mixture for the needs of a cold engine.

If the exhaust continues to shoot out black smoke, then you're burning too much gas in proportion to air. It's an expensive condition because the car is not only guzzling gasoline, but it also could cause a restriction in the catalytic converter, leading to even more expensive repairs.

The problem could be as uncomplicated as a dirty air filter. Since you've made the effort to learn where everything is, lift up the hood and pop out the air filter for a little inspection. If it's really dirty, just hop on over to the auto parts store and buy a new one. Either take the old one with you for match-up, or go armed with the pertinent information: year, model, engine size, and the like of your car.

The black smoke also may be caused by the carburetor if the choke butterfly is faulty or adjusted improperly. If your car has a fuel-injection system instead of a carburetor, the black smoke could be a sign of a system malfunction, or there could be a computer problem.

White Smoke

Billowy white smoke from the tailpipe is caused by one of two things:

1. Moisture is in the system. It might have gotten there via a blown head gasket, a cracked engine head, or a cracked block. These are all serious problems and a job best left for the professionals. Don't ignore the white smoke, because it won't take long for moisture to cause performance problems in the engine.

2. The car is burning transmission fluid in the engine. Sounds pretty weird, right? But it can happen on any automatic transmission that uses a *vacuum modulator.* That's a control device on the outside of the transmission that uses engine vacuum to move a valve inside the transmission. If the diaphragm in the modulator ruptures, the engine vacuum sucks the transmission fluid through a vacuum line and right into the intake manifold. Then it goes into the combustion chamber with the fuel vapor and burns.

If the level of your transmission fluid goes down with no apparent leaks, and at the same time the tailpipe's billowing white smoke, take the car to the repair shop for a new vacuum modulator.

By the way, don't mistake steam for white smoke. Steam only appears around the engine; the white smoke we're talking about here will come from the exhaust system. I mention this because while the white smoke is basically harmless, the steam can cause a serious burn.

Seeing really is believing. Whether you're on a scouting trip or a road trip, keep an eye out for clues.

Do You Hear What I Hear?

O kay, pop quiz time:

Your car starts to give off a horrible squealing sound. You:

A. panic

B. figure unless parts start falling off the car, it's something you can live with

C. turn up the radio loud enough to drown it out

If you answered A, B, or C you failed the quiz. This is a trick question because the correct answer is D: Read this next section very carefully.

Anytime your car makes an unusual sound, it's sending out important audio clues and paying attention can save you big bucks. Some noises are normal, so once again take the time to get acquainted with your car and learn its quirks. If you suddenly notice an unusual knock, ping, bang, or clang, it's time to turn off the radio and do a little investigating.

Backfire

If a spark plug fires while a valve is open, your car will let out a big scary noise that actually sounds like a gunshot. Don't mess around with this one yourself. Let a professional handle the problem, and soon too, because a backfire through the carburetor could start a fire, and a backfire through the exhaust system might manage to blow a hole in your muffler.

Clacking

This noise is similar to the steady clack-clack-clacking of a sewing machine, and it comes from parts located in the lower part of the engine called *valve lifters* or from *rocker arms* at the top of the engine inside the valve cover. A series of valves open and close to allow fuel vapor in and exhaust gases out, and hydraulic lifters move the valves. I've already mentioned a couple of the problems you could run into if you don't faithfully change your oil according to the schedule suggested in your owner's manual, and valve lifter clacking is another one to add to the list.

I wouldn't worry about a clacking sound if the noise disappears after the engine runs for a few minutes, or if the noise is slight and never seems to change. I've known cars that have lived their entire lifetimes with lifter noises. But if the noise occurs suddenly and gets progressively louder, get it to the repair shop immediately because it's possible you're headed for a valve job costing several hundred dollars.

Clicking

Most of the people who come to me complaining about "clicking" sounds are owners of front-wheel-drive vehicles, and the clicking occurs most commonly when they're negotiating sharp turns. It's the result of worn bearings in a CV joint, and the noise should send you straight to the repair shop. If you don't treat it, the sound will just get louder and louder until you have a broken axle and a tow truck driver will be charging you for a trip to the shop.

Four-wheel-drive vehicles also exhibit this clicking for the same reason, but not as commonly as the front-wheel drives.

Clunking and Clanging

Some sounds are hard to describe, but this one sounds exactly like the word: *clunk!*

You may hear it if you step hard on the accelerator and then let up. In this scenario it's usually caused by a broken engine mount, and that can be replaced by the pros. Since the engine mount cannot hold the engine down, torque is actually able to lift it. When you decelerate, gravity takes over and the engine just drops back into place with a *clunk*.

You'll also hear a clunk if there's some slack in the drive line.

Maybe it happens when you first put the car in gear, or you might hear it when you're cruising in high gear, decelerate, then step on the gas pedal again. This type of clunking is common in cars that just naturally have more slack, particularly if the clunk is very slight. I wouldn't worry about this unless the sound becomes severe.

Growling or Groaning on Turns

An old gasoline commercial claimed using its fuel was like having a "tiger in your tank," but that's not the kind of growl I'm referring to here. This growling will usually be accompanied by difficulty turning the steering wheel, and the culprit is a low level of fluid in the power steering reservoir. You can add power steering fluid to stop the noise, but it will only be a temporary fix unless a mechanic determines why the system is leaking in the first place.

Hissing

A leaking vacuum hose is the most common cause of a hissing sound. Listen for this noise when the car is idling, that is, when the car is stopped but the engine is running. Your car will idle more roughly or heavily if a vacuum hose is broken or if it's come off of its port.

If you've got a good ear you can probably handle this problem. Lift the hood and see if you can trace the hissing to a certain area of the engine. If you locate the source of the noise, turn off the engine and look for a broken vacuum hose or pop a dislodged one back into place.

If you are unable to fix this on your own, don't just live with the condition, let a professional check it out. Loss of vacuum leads to a rough-running engine.

Knock and Ping

Think about the sound glass bottles make when they rattle together. That's what I mean by pinging. The pinging sound could be accompanied by a knocking too, and it occurs whenever you accelerate heavily. This noise is caused by an engine combustion problem, something you may have heard mechanics refer to as "spark knock." It happens when compressed gas vapor ignites from the compression at the same time the spark gets there. In short, it's a double detonation. Low octane gasoline also causes pinging. (See sidebar, page 176.)

Solve pinging by trying a simple solution first: Just head to the gas station and fill up the tank with high-octane fuel. If the pinging persists, have it checked by a professional because prolonged pinging eventually will cause engine wear.

If you have an older car and it pings occasionally when you accelerate on a steep grade, just ignore the noise. Older cars may have a carbon buildup in the cylinders, increasing the compression, and while the pinging might stop with a higher-octane gas, few people want to pay the extra expense.

Rapping

A little rapraprapping can quickly become a loud, steady banghangbanging, almost as if someone were under the hood hitting the engine with a hammer. Turn the car off immediately, because a noise like this indicates a serious problem. Your engine could have a bad rod bearing or might even be ready to throw a rod. The connecting rod is what connects the piston to the crankshaft, and if it fails it can knock a hole right through the engine wall. Talk about big-bucks repairs—this one can run into the thousands!

Rattle

If your car sounds as if you have tin cans on a string trailing behind you, I'd say you could describe the sound as a rattle. Rattles are caused by loose parts that shake with the vehicle's motion and hit other parts. The most common rattles are caused by loose exhaust parts, but body parts such as bumper guards or brackets are capable of producing a rattle as well. The good news is that rattles are usually easy to track

Unraveling the Riddle of Octane

Many people believe octane measures the quality or power capabilities of gasoline, but that's incorrect. Octane is the measurement of a gasoline's resistance to detonation or pinging, although factors such as temperature and humidity, driving conditions, and a malfunctioning cooling system affect octane abilities too.

Octane requirements vary from engine to engine, so only use what's recommended in your owner's manual. We live in a society conditioned to think more equals better, so many people purchase a higher-octane gas than they really need or, on the flip side, try to save money by using a lower octane than their car requires. If you buy higher you're wasting your money, and if you buy lower, poor performance increases operating costs, so stick with the manufacturer's recommendation.

down. Head to the repair shop and let your technician tackle the problem.

Roaring

If your mild-mannered car suddenly sounds like a hot rod, and if the roar becomes deafening when you accelerate, you probably have a hole in one of the pipes or the muffler in the exhaust system. Get the car to a repair shop immediately, because while the condition is not harmful to the car, any exhaust leak could allow carbon monoxide to seep into the passenger area, and that's *very* harmful to you.

Another reason you don't want to let this situation linger: In most states you could be issued a citation for noise pollution if your vehicle issues loud exhaust sounds.

Singing, Humming, and Howling

These kinds of problems can be very musical and come in a lot of different pitches. While it might be amusing at first to have your own little symphony on wheels, you'll be singing the blues when the repair shop sends you the bill. In any event, these melodic malfunctions are usually caused by dry or worn-out bearings.

Bearings in alternators, air conditioners, and transmissions are generally high pitched and produce more of a singing or whining sound, and the faster the engine runs the higher pitched the sound becomes.

Wheel bearings vary in tone, and humming comes from the rear-end bearings. This hum will change pitch on acceleration and deceleration, and it will be most noticeable on a straight, smooth road. A rear-end hum should be checked immediately by your auto technician, because a noise like this could be a result of a low lubricant level, and that means a leak somewhere. Catch the noise quickly and you can fix the leak, no big deal. Continue driving and you will destroy the rear end. How would you like to face a repair bill of $500 to $1,000?

Squeaking and Chirping

The key here is to pay attention to *when* the car is making the noise. If the squeaking is slight and occurs only when you're driving on a bumpy road, it may indicate dry parts in the steering or suspension systems. The solution here is a good dose of lubrication. (See Chapter 5.)

If the squeak or chirp occurs in rhythm and gets louder when you drive around bends, the problem may lie in a dry universal joint. A bad universal joint is not too expensive to replace, so take the car to the repair shop. You can't just repack the joint with grease, because once you hear the noise, however slight, the damage is already done and the joint has to be replaced.

Squealing and Screeching

If a high-pitched, rhythmic squeal occurs when you first start the engine, you could have loose fan belts or belts that are drying out. The noise may stop after a short time, or it could continue indefinitely. One indication that the problem is in the fan belt is if the squeal gets worse when you accelerate or on low-speed turns and is accompanied by a jerking reaction in your steering wheel.

A squealing fan belt isn't a big deal. Try an adjustment or take a trip down to your local auto parts store and buy a can of belt dressing. Follow the simple directions listed on the can and spray the lubricant directly onto the belts. But this is a temporary measure. If the squeal continues, *do not* continue to add the dressing, because with repeated use it really gums up the pulleys. Eventually you'll end up taking the car to the repair shop anyhow, and if the auto tech has to scrape all that stuff off the pulley, it won't do anything positive to your repair bill (to say nothing of what it will do to the auto tech's mood).

Thumping

Let's leave the garage for a second and pretend you're in the laundry room. When you run a washing machine with an uneven load and it enters the spin cycle, you'll hear a rhythmic thumping noise. Your car can give off the same kind of sound, which will change in frequency as the car's speed increases or decreases.

Under these circumstances, a thumping noise indicates a problem with one of the tires, which might be developing a bubble. Sometimes the problem is inside the tire; then you won't be able to see it, so you'll have to rely on a professional for help. Continued driving with this kind of problem could lead to a blowout, an emergency situation you certainly want to avoid.

Ticking

A cracked flywheel causes a rhythmic ticking sound when the car is idling. Depending on the size of the crack, the sound varies from slight to very, very loud, but as soon as you accelerate and start moving the ticking should disappear. Still, you need to take this one to the repair shop because, left untreated, the flywheel could break completely, and you'd have to pay for a tow to the repair shop.

Noises When Braking

Whether we're talking about brake performance or unusual noises during braking, it's a clue to head to the professionals. Suspicious brake sounds should send you straight to the shop.

Grinding

Nothing is guaranteed to make you shudder faster than the sound of metal scraping against metal. If you hear it when you use the brakes, the probable cause is a badly worn brake lining. As always, with any problem in the brake system, get your car to the repair shop immediately.

By the way, your transmission can make a grinding sound too, but it still requires a trip to the repair shop.

Squeaks or Whispering

Some cars make this noise with normal braking action and it's not a problem, but watch out for sounds associated with the brake-wear sensors. Unless your car has always made a little squeak or whisper when you use the brakes, get it checked by a professional.

Car noises are funny things because often the sound travels, so even though you've read these descriptions you might still find it difficult to diagnose the problem. If that's the case, don't just drop off the car at the repair shop and hope for the best. You'll be a tremendous help to the auto technician if you come in prepared to answer the questions on this checklist, and it might even reduce your bill because the mechanic will spend less time eliminating possible causes.

Sound Effects Checklist:

✔ Is the sound present when the car is moving, sitting still, or both?

✔ Is the noise louder when the car is hot or cold?

✔ Does the noise only occur when the car is going in a certain direction (e.g., forward, backward)?

✔ Does the engine have to be running in order to hear the noise?

✔ Does it occur on a bend or a straight road?

✔ Does the sound change with speed?

✔ Do you hear the noise when you accelerate or decelerate?

✔ Do you only get the noise on a bumpy road?

Look Before You Leak: Matching Liquids to Their Locations

It's a fact of life that some cars leak. The source of the leak could indicate a serious problem, or it might just mean a messy garage floor, but either way you want to take care of it as soon as possible. If you can distinguish between the leaks that run up a red flag and the others that can wait, I guarantee your life will be whole lot easier.

I guess, technically, you could say this is something that could have been included under "Recognizing Problems by Sight" or even "Recognizing Problems by Smell" because a leak may leave both kinds of clues. But they are such a common occurrence and there's so much to say about them, I feel leaks deserve an entire section of their own. Once again, understanding your car's systems is the key to identifying a leak because the color, consistency, and location of the leaking component all aid in the diagnosis.

Antifreeze

Color: Green

Location: Front of car

Coolant, which is what we call the mixture of antifreeze and water, circulates throughout the engine dissipating heat and acting as a rust inhibitor. After picking up the heat, it goes through the radiator, where it is cooled, and then it returns to the hot area. Coolant is usually green, and, even though it doesn't look like oil, it feels oily to the touch. Some cooling systems may lose their green color and have a rusty look. (See sidebar, page 182.)

Coolant leaks can be found almost anywhere under the engine area—from the radiator up front to the rear of the engine. If the coolant leak is severe, it won't take long for the engine to overheat. In fact, many customers have told me they weren't even aware they were losing coolant until the engine overheated. Don't be intimidated by a coolant leak; you probably can identify the source of the leak on your own, and believe it or not, the first place to look is not in your car—it's on your garage floor.

Inspect your garage floor for puddles of green antifreeze. If the puddle is near the front of the car, check the radiator for leaks. Also check the radiator hoses, upper and lower, and the water pump, which is located directly behind the fan. A leak from the heater hose could cause drips farther back or even leave little green puddles on top of the engine.

Sometimes you won't be able to identify the source of the leak unless the engine is running, but don't let that scare you off. Just raise the hood, start the engine, and watch where the puddle develops or where steam starts to rise.

Rusty Antifreeze

I f your coolant appears rusty, it's picking up some of the rust from internal parts of your car. Because antifreeze is a rust inhibitor, it's a bad idea to run your cooling system with water only. Sometimes people will skip the antifreeze if they live in climates that don't present temperature dangers, but then they're losing the rust-inhibitor benefits of the antifreeze.

If a hose is to blame for the leak, replace it. If you're not feeling so handy that day, I advise you to let your auto technician handle the repair instead. Either way, fix the problem immediately; it's a lot easier to take care of a coolant leak than it is to take care of a car that's overheated.

I mentioned one fact about coolant earlier but it bears repeating: Antifreeze is a deadly poison, and even a small dose can kill a child or pet. Its light-green color might make it look like lime soda to a kid, and it even has a sweet taste, so always take extra precautions when handling antifreeze, and store it in a locked cabinet.

Engine Oil

Color: Black or gray

Location: Front of car

Engine oil leaks leave black or gray puddles anywhere under the engine area. If you don't make a habit of looking at the garage floor for leaks (and in that case my advice is that you *do* make a habit of it), an indicator light on your dash may be the first sign that you're low on engine oil. The "engine oil pressure" light will flicker red, or the oil pressure gauge will register low pressure.

An automobile engine has a bunch of different seals and gaskets, and any one of them has the potential to spring a leak. But a puddle on the floor or a light on the dash isn't the only signs of an engine oil leak; you also might smell a burning, hot odor if the oil leaks onto the exhaust system.

Deciding how to handle an engine oil leak calls for a little common sense. If your car is leaking a lake of oil every time you park and you have to add oil frequently, then steer toward the repair shop right away. But if the oil spots are small and you rarely if ever have to add oil, there's no cause for panic. Older cars with a lot of mileage are going to leave an oil spot here and there, and you'll have to decide for yourself if you'd rather pay for a repair or put up with the small task of cleaning the garage floor. To tell you the truth, it's the kind of problem I'd tell you to live with.

Transmission Fluid

Color: Red (If clean)

Location: Front or middle of car

Automatic transmissions are hydraulically operated, and if the car starts to leak transmission fluid, eventually the level becomes low enough to cause performance problems. The initial sign would be a delay or hesitation when you first put the selector lever into gear when the car is cold. Standard transmissions can leak too, but with less frequency than automatics.

A leak from the transmission can be tricky to diagnose because both the location and color of the leak vary. Let's deal with the variance in color first. Clean automatic transmission fluid is bright red like cherry soda pop, but if the car has some kind of impending internal problem, or you've neglected routine fluid changes, the color appears yellow-tan to black. This is when it gets difficult to determine if the leak is transmission fluid or engine oil.

I'm going to let you in on a simple trick from the professionals about how to tell the difference:

1. Get a sample of the leaking fluid on a paper towel.

2. Pull out the engine oil dipstick (it may or may not be labeled), and let a few drops fall onto the paper towel.

3. Collect a few drips from the transmission dipstick (also may or may not be labeled).

4. Compare the colors of the fluids to see which one matches the leak.

If you still can't determine the source of the leak by color, then move on to the location of the leak for more clues. Transmissions in rear-wheel-drive cars are located directly behind the engine in the middle of the car, but even in these vehicles it's possible to leak transmission fluid under the engine area. That's because small lines carry the transmission fluid to a special compartment in the radiator to be cooled and returned to the transmission, and some of these lines develop leaks. Front-wheel-drive transmissions are located beside the engine under the hood and can leak in the same general area as the engine.

Transmission leaks are a job for the pros, so it's off to the repair shop again. Your responsibility in the leaking transmission scenario is to be sure to keep the fluid level up until the leak is repaired.

Power Steering Fluid

Color: Varies red to brown

Location: Under engine area

Power steering fluid can leak from a number of different places, but all of them will be under the general area of the engine. The fluid can be red or pinkish like new transmission fluid, or it can be different shades of brown. Whether the leak is from a power steering hose or one of the integral operating parts of the steering system, the problem requires a professional for repairs.

The first sign that you're low on power steering fluid may be a growling sound when you make an extreme turn. The power steering reservoir has a dipstick under the hood for checking levels, and once again, on most cars, it's labeled so you can find it easily. (See Chapter 4.)

Rear-End Grease

Color: Brownish

Location: Center between rear wheels

The first sign of a low fluid level in the rear end might be a faint howling sound on a straight, smooth road that changes pitch on acceleration or deceleration. If you notice this sound, check the garage floor in the center between the rear wheels. If you spot an accumulation of brownish-looking grease, the problem is probably a faulty seal on the front of the rear axle assembly, which is where the driveshaft goes in.

If the grease level gets low in the rear axle assembly, the bearings and gears will wear without lubrication, resulting in one pretty expensive failure. Your best bet to prevent it *and* stop the howling noise is to let an auto technician immediately add more grease and repair any problem with the seal.

Gasoline and Brake Fluid

Color: Nondescript

Location: Anywhere

The color and location here are pretty discouraging: fluids that don't have a color, and a location that could be anywhere. But the smell will give away these two fluids every time, because both have unmistakable odors. If your garage floor is sporting a puddle that defies identification, wipe it up with a paper towel and give it a sniff.

Undoubtedly you'd recognize the smell of gasoline, but you might

Cleaning Stains from the Garage Floor

I can make a couple of compelling arguments for cleaning up the stains on your garage floor. The first is: Stains look terrible. But even if you don't think neatness counts, think about this: Once you've repaired the leaks, you'll want to be able to tell if any new ones occur, and how can you do that if your floor is covered with old stains? I've got a couple of tried-and-true solutions for garage floor stains, and if they work in a professional repair shop, you can bet they'll work on your floor at home.

If you just happen to spill a lot of oil and you don't let it sit on the floor for a long time, then it's easy to clean. Visit your auto parts store for a drying compound called Oil-Dry, which you can pour directly on the spill. The compound is a lot like coarse sand, absorbing oil to the point that you can then just grab a broom and sweep the whole mess right up. If you don't want another bag lying around in the garage, then here's a little tip: *cat box filler* works just as well! Many kinds even have the advantage of having a deodorant in them, so your floor will smell better after the spill. (Just be careful your cat doesn't get into the pile and think he's found himself a new bathroom!)

If you've had a long-term leak under your car and the stain looks sort of thick and nasty, pour on the drying compound or the cat box filler and let it sit for five days. Then sweep up the compound and sprinkle the area with laundry detergent. Add some hot water and scrub with a stiff broom. Once the floor dries, it will look as good as new.

not have had the opportunity to smell brake fluid, which has a very strong and penetrating odor. The next time you're at the repair shop, ask your favorite technician to let you take a whiff of brake fluid. I guarantee you'll never forget the experience.

Gasoline can leak from the gas tank itself (usually located at the rear of the car), from fuel lines, the fuel pump, or from either the carburetor or fuel-injection system on top of the engine.

Brake fluid leaks occur at the wheels, where it might run down the inside of the tire. Brake lines and hoses that carry the brake fluid to the four wheels also have the potential to leak, as does the master cylinder. If you find an unidentifiable clear puddle on your garage floor *and* you notice a spongy, soft brake pedal that has to be pumped to stop, you can assume the problem is leaking brake fluid.

Air Conditioner Condensation

Color: Clear

Location: Under engine area, usually right side

On a hot, muggy day you might park your car and come back to find a puddle of water under it. If it's a day with particularly high humidity, you'll find something that's more like a pool than a puddle, but don't panic. Chances are this is just unavoidable condensation from your air conditioner, so don't embarrass yourself by rushing to the repair shop.

Make a habit of scouting the floor where your car is parked for signs of leaks. (Don't let funny looks from the neighbors deter you.) One word of advice though: Don't be fooled by *another car's leaks*. Use a public parking area and it's possible to park in a space that had a leaking car before you. In a situation like this, park your car in a clean area and watch it before you rush to the shop.

Occasionally a leak is difficult to pinpoint even at the repair shop. We auto repair people may know what fluid is leaking and still have trouble figuring out just what it's leaking from. Be an understanding and helpful customer, and if you really want to impress the mechanics, leave a piece of cardboard under the car the night before you take it to the shop. If you deliver not only the leaking car but also a sample of the leaking fluid and information about its location, you can bet you'll be named "Customer of the Year."

"I Think It's the ... or, Maybe the ... Uhhh ..."

I'm the kind of person who likes a lot of logic in my life. Whenever I have to diagnose a car problem, I follow all the logical routes and the answer will almost always present itself.

Almost always . . .

Occasionally we mechanics come across some sort of miscellaneous problem that defies logical explanation. And believe me, it's just as frustrating for the auto technician as it is for the owner of the car. I've listed some of those problems here because they really don't fit in the categories I've already discussed, but they can't be left out either.

Poor Gas Mileage

"I just filled up the tank last Saturday and I'm already out of gas!"

Sound familiar? Many people complain about poor gas mileage, but the fact is, most of them don't have an accurate idea of what the gas mileage is or should be in the first place. If you're concerned about your car's fuel costs, check the mileage accurately before you resort to any heavy-duty worrying.

The first and most obvious way to determine expected gas mileage is to look at the car manufacturer's specs. A lot of times I've heard people complain that their new cars aren't getting good gas mileage when in fact they're getting exactly what the manufacturer predicted. But these new car owners are comparing gas consumption to that of their *old* cars, which might have gotten better mileage.

The other method for determining your gas mileage is a matter of simple math:

If **A** = the mileage on the odometer prior to filling the gas tank, and **B** = the odometer's mileage after you use up that gas, and **C** = the exact amount of gasoline you put in the tank.

Then $\dfrac{\mathbf{B} - \mathbf{A}}{\mathbf{C}}$ = **Gas Mileage**

Whether that number can be considered "good" or "bad" depends on a lot of factors, including what kind of vehicle you have and where you drive it. So let's suppose that you checked your owner's manual and it predicts your car should get 27 miles per gallon (mpg). But when you figured out how much your car is actually getting, the number is a lot lower. With a little thought and checking—and, of course, with a little common sense—you will discover why your car is a gas hog.

Your car might be consuming too much gas for a lot of different reasons, all of them fitting into one of three categories: driver control, car problems, and environmental factors. Read them all and see if any, or all, could be the logical path to solving your problem.

Driver Control

You may not realize it, but as a driver you have a tremendous amount of control over how much fuel your car consumes. First, think about accessories. Every accessory on a car demands just a little gasoline to keep it going. The biggest guzzler is the air conditioner, which can cause gas mileage to drop as much as 2.5 miles per gallon. So at low speeds, roll down those window and let the breeze cool you instead.

Notice I said *at low speeds*. Believe it or not, you'll actually use *more* gas if you drive at high speeds with the windows down because of wind resistance. Cars are designed with aerodynamics in mind.

The amount of weight you carry in your car makes a difference too. For every additional 100 pounds on board you lose two-tenths of a mile per gallon, so don't just stick to your diet, take some time to clear all that extra clutter out of the car's trunk. And keep this factor in mind on long vacations, because a trunk filled with luggage affects gas mileage during the trip.

But accessories and the weight in your car can't even begin to compare to the real biggie: your own driving habits. You reach a point in speed—usually between 50 to 60 mph, depending on your car's design—when gas mileage is at its peak. Driving any faster only decreases the number of miles you get per gallon. This is another good argument against speeding.

Jackrabbit starts, the kind where you take off by slamming the gas pedal to the floor, will also cause your car to drink gas, as will hurry-up-and-stop driving. If you accelerate right up to the red light and then jam on the brakes at the last minute, not only are you guzzling gas but you're also doing a real job on the brakes.

To get the best gas mileage, drive with an eye on what's coming up. If you see a traffic light turn to yellow, take your foot off the gas pedal and coast the rest of the way to the stop. Avoid long periods of idling, which requires a richer fuel mixture. And when it's time to move again, take off with a gentle, even increase in acceleration. The same holds true when passing on the highway; cruise with a gradual acceleration instead of a sudden spurt of speed. This kind of driving is best for gas mileage and for the other systems of your car as well—and no coincidence, it's also the safer way to drive.

Car Problems

To lump a lot of possibilities into one, let's say that a car in need of a tune-up or performance check will use more gas. Any problem with the fuel system, carburetor, or fuel injection will affect mileage, as will a dirty air filter and underinflated tires. A bad thermostat in the cooling system prevents the engine from warming up quickly, and a cold engine burns more fuel than a warm one. And finally, a car in need of a front-end alignment uses more gas because a bad toe-in adjustment causes one tire to drag around curves.

A dragging brake will steal a few miles per gallon, and it's not at all unusual to have a parking brake that doesn't fully release. If you feel resistance, like you're pulling a heavy load, you should check your car for a parking brake problem. Park on a grade, put the car in neutral, and see if the car drifts. If it does not drift, the likely suspect is a dragging parking brake. (Continue to drive with this condition and you'll damage the transmission.)

Transmissions affect the amount of gas your car consumes too. For years it's been common knowledge that manual transmissions use less gas than automatics. That's because the driver can shift out of lower gears quickly and into higher gears where less gas is required. But the good news is that with newer automatics and their computer-controlled shifts, the gap is closing. In fact, these days the gas mileage of a well-operating automatic is nearly equal to that of a manual.

You'll be able to tell if your automatic transmission is having a performance problem because it will slip (the engine races but the car doesn't move), or it will shift up from lower gears at higher speeds, and both of these conditions will cause gas mileage to nosedive. What does this tell you? Fix those little problems fast or else you won't just face the cost of repair, you'll face increased operating costs too.

Environmental Factors

Here we're talking about terrain—as in Kansas, with long stretches of flat, smooth, straight roads, versus New York City, with twists and turns and traffic lights at the end of every block. Long, flat, straight roads are ideal for fuel economy. Shift into high gear or overdrive and you can go for miles on the least amount of gas. Hilly or mountainous roads or lots of in-the-city driving call for lower gears, varying speeds, and lots of stops and starts. The difference is so great that manufacturers even give two estimates for miles per gallon ratings: one for the highway and one for the city.

Dieseling

Back in the 1960s, when my three kids were young, we had a station wagon with a dieseling problem. That's when you turn off the key but your car continues to run, kind of shaking and gasping its way to an eventual stop. In fact, I wouldn't even say it stops. It looks a lot more like the car shudders and dies.

Well, this station wagon of mine was so bad that it would actually do this coughing and sputtering act for several long, torturous minutes, a condition I found so embarrassing that I would vault out of the car and run away from it before anyone had the chance to see me. But not my kids. They found it terribly amusing and always wanted to hang back and watch. In fact, they bragged that our car could do "the Twist." (This was in the era of Chubby Checker.)

Fuel injection, superior gasoline, and better ignition systems have all but eliminated dieseling in today's cars, but if you drive an early model you don't have to live with it. Try turning the engine off while the transmission is still in gear and then move the lever to "park." The lower RPM of the engine when in gear will usually cause the engine to stop when you turn off the key. But (you're probably noticing a trend by now) you don't just want the temporary fix, you want to know what's causing the problem in the first place. Here are some of the possibilities:

✔ The engine idle may be too high, the engine could be running too hot, or you could be using a gasoline with too low an octane.

✔ The car may have a buildup of carbon in the combustion chambers. The carbon remains hot enough to glow and ignite the gas vapor even after the key is turned off.

You'll be able to tell, by sound and feel, if the idle is too high or the engine too hot, and the best remedy for that is a drive to the repair shop. If those aren't the causes of your dieseling, try a higher octane gas. If you still have the dieseling, move on to the next likely culprit, the carbon buildup. If most of your driving is the stop-start city kind, a nice long drive on a highway will clear the cylinders of the carbon. In fact, if your car is city-bound, I would recommend the occasional Sunday drive even if you don't have a dieseling problem. It's a good preventive measure for the car and, I might add, not a bad stress-reliever for the driver!

No Heat from the Heater

Some drivers from warmer climates might be inclined to skip over this section, but if you're one of those drivers and you're still reading, I'm going to ask you to imagine this scenario: Dead of winter, early morning, and you're driving down the road in a freezing cold car. Your teeth chatter in time to the song on the radio, your nose is dripping, and you grip the steering wheel with fingers that feel like little icicles. You are thinking *A cup of coffee would be nice, not for drinking but for drizzling over my frostbitten hands.*

You drivers who live in cold climates don't have to imagine this. You know all too well what it feels like. This is what we face when the car's heater goes out, which usually happens in one of two ways. First, the fan may be blowing, but it's giving off cold air instead of warm; or second, the heat may be there, but the blower isn't working. Either one of those problems is mighty frustrating when the temperature is in the twenties.

Heat for the heater is provided by the cooling system, which circulates coolant through a heater core. The fan blows the heat from that core into the passenger compartment. When you first start the car, the coolant will be cold and the fan will blow chilly air, but it should heat up in a matter of minutes, thanks to the *thermostat.*

The thermostat is a valve located at the top of the engine at the upper radiator hose. A temperature-sensitive spring controls a valve, which is closed when the engine is cold. When the valve is closed, coolant can't circulate, but as the engine warms up to efficient operating temperature, so does the coolant, causing the temperature-sensitive spring to expand and open the valve. Hot coolant circulates throughout the system, including the heater core, and *voilá,* heat in the passenger compartment.

But what if the thermostat is faulty? What if the little valve doesn't close? In cold weather it takes forever for the engine to warm up, and you most likely will arrive at your destination long before you get any heat from the heater. Thermostats can also stick the other way, closed; in that case your car will overheat very quickly. (To determine if your thermostat is broken, see Chapter 4.)

The good news is that thermostats are an inexpensive repair, so don't risk the frostbite. Take your car to the shop. If the blower itself doesn't blow, or the switch seems to be broken, let the technician check it out. But remember one other possibility before you head to the repair shop: Your car might be low on coolant. A low level prevents adequate flow through the heater core, and you end up getting less or no heat. You can add more coolant yourself, but remember how one thing always leads to another? If the coolant level is low you can't just add more and forget about it. You have to determine why the car leaked the coolant in the first place, so do a little investigating and go to the shop armed with information.

Speedometer Doesn't Work

I can think of a few times in my life when I wished the speedometer *was* broken—like the times I get caught speeding. But other than that it's a pretty inconvenient condition. Later-model cars have electronically controlled speedometers, but if you have an early-model car and you face a broken speedometer, its source is one of three possibilities:

1. The speedometer "head" in the dash could be bad.

2. The gears that pick up the speed reading from your transmission may be broken or worn.

3. The problem may be with the cable connecting the transmission to the speedometer.

Your auto technician can determine the culprit by disconnecting the speedometer at the transmission. There's a small gear on the end of the cable at the transmission, and if you turn it by hand, you should see the numbers register on the speedometer. That means the speedometer unit itself is okay, so next the tech will shine a flashlight in the speedometer housing opening on the transmission to check the wear on the inner gear. A broken cable is quite obvious because you'll be able to pull the inner cable right out of the outer housing.

Lights Don't Work

When a light doesn't work in your house, your first instinct is to change the burned-out lightbulb. Well, the same holds true for your car, and

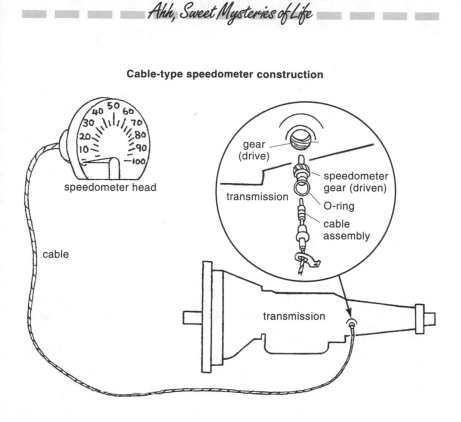

Cable-type speedometer construction

speedometer head

gear (drive)

transmission

speedometer gear (driven)

O-ring

cable assembly

transmission

cable

in many cases this is so simple anyone can do it. Look carefully to see what has to be removed to get to the bulb and how to reinsert the new one, and note the type of replacement bulb you'll need. Then head to the auto parts store, buy a replacement, and change the bulb. A few tips:

✔ Never touch the glass part of the bulb, especially if your hands are dirty. Your hands can leave an oil behind that will burn on the bulb.

✔ Be extremely careful if you are handling halogen bulbs because they have pressurized gas inside and they can burst if you scratch or drop the bulb.

✔ Before you start replacing bulbs, take a good look at the area. I've known customers who complained about dim or burned-out lights when the problem was just a bulb that was so dirty the light couldn't get through!

Unfortunately, not every case is so simple. Sometimes the problem might be caused by a faulty switch or a bad electrical ground. These go beyond your average amateur repairs, so let the techs check it out.

Limp Mode

Does this phrase conjure up the image of a car hobbling along on crutches? In a way, that's exactly what "limp mode" is. It's a new feature on sophisticated later-model cars with extensive electronic controls, designed because the cars have the potential for a complete shutdown, and if that happens the limp mode takes over. Fuel and timing are no longer controlled by the computer, the engine runs but with very little power, and the transmission will usually stay in second gear or, sometimes, third.

The idea is to give the car just enough power and control to "limp" to the repair shop. Once it's there a technician uses sophisticated electronic tools to figure out what went wrong in the computer or any of the other involved components. Without the limp mode feature, you'd be in for a lot of lost time and an expensive tow truck for something as minor as a loose electrical connection.

Cars are getting more and more sophisticated by the day, and many of them are designed to alert you to a problem long before you ever have to use the limp mode. The dash of the Cadillac, for instance, flashes the warning "check engine soon" when a problem first develops. Ignore it and you'll soon see "service engine soon" flashing on the dash; ignore that and you'll get the message "service engine now." Don't gripe if you end up in limp mode after ignoring so many warnings, because breaking down then is your own fault.

Idiot Lights

Those "check engine soon" and "service engine now" lights I just talked about have a name: idiot lights. It's not a very polite-sounding term. In fact, it originated out of the belief that you'd have to be an idiot to ignore them. They used to flash red but with no message; today's cars are really detailed with plenty of printed messages on the dash, warning drivers of an impending problem.

Some cars are equipped with gauges to show temperature, oil pressure, or electrical charging data. In my opinion those kinds of signals are more about status than they are about service, because although they sure look impressive, your everyday driver wouldn't really know what to do with the data. I prefer the lights that offer more commonly needed information.

When you first turn the key in the ignition, before starting the car, all the lights will be red. Once the engine starts, the lights go out. If any of the lights continue to flash red warnings, how fast you should react depends on which of the following lights is flashing:

Charge

The alternator, or "charge" light, turns red when the charging system is not creating enough electrical current. When that happens the battery is making up the difference, and in older cars that only means the battery will be drained and eventually—when you turn off the car—you won't be able to get it to start again unless you jump the battery. That's inconvenient, but it's not really an emergency situation.

With newer cars the problem is more serious because computer-controlled systems can malfunction on low voltage. Depending on the problem and the car, your engine might quit running altogether or it might throw the system into limp mode. The cause of the charging problem might be as simple as a loose belt, but an internal problem with the alternator is more serious. So when the red light flashes, have the car checked immediately.

Brakes

The first thing to do when the brake light flashes is check to make sure that you did indeed release the parking brake. If you have released it and the light is still flashing red, the hydraulic system might be low. Have your auto technician check and add more brake fluid as necessary, then determine why the brake fluid leaked. Don't drive the car if the brake pedal feels at all mushy. For the sake of safety, have it towed to the shop.

If you have an antilock break system (ABS brakes), both a red light and an amber light will be on for a few seconds after starting the car. Once the lights go out it means the system is fully operational. If the lights stay on, let a technician investigate the problem.

Engine Oil Pressure

Check the level of the engine oil at the first sight of this red warning light. (See Chapter 5.) A low level of engine oil is the most common cause of low oil pressure, so if you fill up the engine the warning light should go off. But, as with all leaks, you have to determine why and from where the engine oil was leaking in the first place. (See Chapter 7, p. 180.)

If you don't find any leaks but the engine oil level continues to drop, it probably means the engine is burning the oil. That's a serious problem. It could be caused by bad rings on the pistons or totally clogged-up oil passages. Your responsibility is to make sure the level is always up even if you have to check and add oil frequently until the problem is solved. This might seem inconvenient, but driving a car that's low on engine oil will result in engine damage, and that's worse than inconvenient, that's expensive! If you find yourself contending with a persistent leak, it's okay to use the cheap oil until you get the car fixed.

If the oil pressure light is red but the engine oil level is *not* low, then your car either truly does have low pressure in the engine or the oil pressure switch is faulty. Either way it has to go to the repair shop, but should you drive it there? Maybe. If the red light flickers only when the engine is idling but goes out as soon as you accelerate, you should have no problem driving it to a nearby shop. But if the light stays on, try driving very gently with light acceleration, and listen for engine noise. If you hear engine noise, any noise at all, call the tow truck. Again, it might be expensive, but it's nothing compared to the cost of replacing the whole engine.

Temperature

The temperature warning light indicates an engine that is running too hot. The first thing to do is cool the engine down and check the coolant level. If it's low, add antifreeze and water. In an emergency you can add water alone, but remember once the crisis is over to get some antifreeze back in the system. (See Chapter 4, p. 61.)

If you're forced to drive a car with a hot engine, at least try to stop at regular intervals to cool down the engine until you can get real help. This condition can result in blown hoses and eventually serious engine damage, such as a cracked engine block.

You wouldn't ignore road signs telling you of hazardous conditions up ahead, so don't ignore your car's cries for help, subtle or otherwise. They don't necessarily mean you're facing an expensive repair. Let an auto technician check a problem when it first turns up, and most likely you've just *prevented* costly trips to the shop.

Service with a Smile

For a long time the automotive repair industry was the wicked stepsister of the repair trade. Mechanics were seen as "grease monkeys" out to make a buck on expensive fraudulent repairs, and it wasn't until a decade or so ago that nonprofit agencies such as the National Car Care Council, Automotive Service Excellence, and the Automotive Information Council succeeded as fairy godmothers. They worked hard to improve the industry's image, and at the same time, advanced technical training and pay scales elevated the workforce. Today I believe most shops are staffed by honest, hardworking businesspeople, but it only takes one unscrupulous act and *bang*, the whole industry is turned into a pumpkin at midnight and we're back to fighting a bad reputation.

I know a lot of customers assume the role of victim in these situations, but it doesn't have to be that way. The biggest step you can take to avoid being cheated is to choose a good shop in the first place. I already told you I think choosing a repair shop is like choosing a doctor. If you told your physician you occasionally had a mild stomachache and the doc responded, "Hmmmmm, sounds like appendicitis. Let's schedule surgery for tomorrow," you'd probably leave the office so fast there'd be skid marks on the path out the door. Most people do some research before they choose a doctor; at the very least, they seek a referral from a friend.

Don't be shy about visiting a shop before your car develops a problem. Look around, ask questions, notice operating procedures and staff attitudes. Any reputable shop would be happy to accommodate you. I believe you'd earn a lot of points in their eyes because you're such a concerned car owner.

Know the Different Types of Repair Shops

T he first step in choosing a repair shop is knowing which kind meets your car's needs. Just as you wouldn't go to a foot doctor to discuss your heart condition, neither would you go to a body shop for an engine tune-up, so let's begin by describing the different kinds of repair shops and the services they provide.

New Car Dealer Service Department

Service departments specialize in only the kinds of cars sold at that particular dealer, basically a plus for you because the technicians are factory-trained and experienced in late-model technology. As long as your car is under factory warranty, you'll have to take it to this kind of service department for repairs. On the negative side, dealership service tends to be more expensive, so once the factory warranty expires, most car owners tend to move on to independent repair shops.

General Repair Shops

General repair shops range in size from the one- or two-mechanic shop to high-volume places owned and operated by corporations, frequently oil or tire companies. One bonus of the small shop is personalized service, since you'll deal with the same technician each time you bring the car in for repairs. The larger corporate-controlled shops are often clean and bright with convenient locations and extended business hours, but they're only as good or as bad as their management and technicians.

In an auto club survey I did a few years back, a random sampling of car owners showed most people prefer the personalized service of a small general repair shop. Later in this chapter I'll give you some guidelines on choosing a repair shop, so you can decide which size shop fits your budget and your lifestyle.

Specialty Shops

Specialty shops are exactly what the name implies, shops that specialize in one particular kind of repair, like my shop, Transmissions by Lucille. Others specialize in exhaust work, engine rebuilding, body work, even auto electrical components such as starters and alternators.

These shops may be independently owned or they could be franchises, but in either case many offer advantages to the car owner. Technicians in a specialty shop are more likely to be educated on the latest repairs and developments since they have to study only one part of the car, and by extension product quality tends to be higher. Prices are also usually competitive.

Evaluate each specialty shop just as you would a general repair shop and make the choice that's right for your car's problem.

Tire Store Shops

Tire shops used to do nothing more than sell tires and perform repairs closely related to tires, such as the occasional front-end alignment or tire balance. Often backed by tire corporations and driven by the need to be more competitive, today many tire stores have branched out to include general repair shop duties. Like the big general repair shops, their quality varies.

Ten-Minute "Anything" Shops

Drive around the suburbs and you're sure to see Ten-Minute Anything Shops on every corner. From oil changes to muffler repair to detailing, a lot of shops—whether franchises or privately owned—promise an assortment of services while you wait. The bonus is convenience and cost.

In the past few years, quick-change oil shops have had a tremendously positive impact on people's perception of this crucial maintenance task. While I'm all for anything that encourages people to maintain the engine oil, don't be blinded by the light of convenience alone, because sometimes these places are staffed with less-experienced technicians. I don't mean to sound negative. I'm just suggesting that you research a quick-service shop as carefully as you would any full-service one.

Parts Company Repair Shops

Repair shops that are offspring of larger parts companies keep popping up around the country. Like the big general repair shops, these outfits are big, bright, clean, and most likely well equipped, but once again, the service will vary depending on the management.

Parts company repair shops are convenient—imagine shopping for your general maintenance products while technicians work on your car—but look for the same kind of quality track record you'd demand in a smaller shop.

State Inspections

This might seem like an odd time to talk about state inspections, right in the middle of talking about different kinds of repair shops. But the reason I'm bringing it up now is because a lot of people are under the impression that a state inspection actually includes checking the performance and condition of everything on the car, and it most definitely does not. All the time I hear customers tell me they can't figure out how a transmission problem developed because "I just had the car inspected."

Twenty-four of the fifty states and Washington, D.C., require periodic inspection of automobiles, and requirements to pass vary. The goal of the state inspection is to ensure your car's safety, not just for you but for other motorists and the environment as well. (Twenty-eight states and Washington, D.C., require emissions testing.) Approved state inspectors check front-end and steering parts, lights and turn signals, windshield wipers, the suspension system, tire tread, and the exhaust system, just to name a few. Problems that don't affect safety, such as a rough-running engine or a radiator leak, wouldn't cause you to be denied an inspection sticker, but if you had a problem with your transmission—if it wouldn't shift into reverse, for instance—it would be considered a safety issue and the car would fail.

Check with an approved state inspection facility in your area for a list of your state's inspection criteria. Follow its guidelines, and keep your inspection sticker current—but don't ever make the mistake of thinking you're sending the car in for a complete checkup.

A Word about Sales Staff

Not only do repair shops differ, so do salespeople, and knowing the difference between two major kinds can save you big bucks. You want to deal with a salesperson who explains a technical diagnosis, describes a list of repairs, and quotes you a price range.

Be wary of merchandisers who hire people trained to sell because most of them work on commission, and they'll get a percentage of what they sell you. Listen for come-on lines designed to intimidate you. If the customer is a woman, the salesperson might play on vulnerability: *"You don't ever drive alone at night in this car, do you?"* The men get something like *"Do you drive your wife and family around in this car?"* If you don't know anything about auto repair, scare tactics like these will send you scrambling for your checkbook, ready to write out any figure they tell you.

If you have a doubt about what you're told your car needs, seek out a second opinion. This is true no matter what type of repair shop you're in. As you perfect your role as the Educated Car Owner, it will be easier to spot illogical diagnoses and to make decisions about what's best for your car.

Choosing a Repair Shop

So now you're able to limit your choices to the shop that's right for your car's condition. You might want to narrow the field even further by considering only shops that are close to your home or that have convenient operating hours, but don't limit your choice to those criteria. You will inevitably discover, the hard way, that convenience rates a distant second to quality. I think one of the best ways to narrow down your choices is to listen to referrals from your friends, family, coworkers, and neighbors. If someone whose opinion you know and trust raves about an honest shop with competent technicians and consistent service, it pays to check it out, even if you do have to travel out of your way to get there.

For the Record . . .

By this stage of the process you might be left with two or three possibilities, so now it's time to research their track records. Several agencies keep records, and I suggest you start with the Better Business Bureau. Inquire if any complaints have ever been lodged against the repair shop and how the problems were resolved. The BBB is a good place to start, but remember, the system has its weaknesses. First, if the business is fairly new, the BBB might not have had enough time to accumulate a track record on the shop. Also, charges against a shop must be submitted in writing, and few people will take the time and effort to file a written complaint after their initial anger subsides.

Your next step would be to contact the Consumer Protection Bureau of your State Attorney General's Office. Not only will that department give information about specific repair shops, it also investigates auto repair complaints and in some cases will assist you in getting compensation. You're off to a good start if neither the BBB or Consumer Protection Agency has any record of complaints against the prospective shop.

Take the Guided Tour

Your final step in the selection process is to visit the shops and trust your own judgment. The first thing that should greet you when you step inside a shop (after a polite receptionist, that is) are ASE certificates on the wall. *ASE* stands for Automotive Service Excellence, a nonprofit group that promotes automotive repair training and offers voluntary testing. Twice a year technicians have the opportunity voluntarily to test their skills in all phases of auto repair and keep up on advancing technology, and ASE certificates on the shop wall demonstrate employee pride and competence.

Seek permission to look around the shop and, as you do, trust your own intuition, observations, and good old common sense. Start with the shop's appearance. Is it clean and orderly with litter-free floors and tools arranged neatly on a hanging wall board? If you go into a dungeonlike shop strewn with broken parts, tools, and soft-drink cans, you can only imagine how they'd treat the inside of your car. If a technician needs a specialty tool to make a difficult repair but can't find it under the discarded boxes and car parts, what do you suppose he'll do? Probably reach for the closest tool he can find, and odds are good it will be a hammer!

Don't get me wrong—no busy repair shop will be immaculate, because, after all, car repair is dirty work. But you can tell the difference between a busy shop with a little operating clutter and one that's swimming in grease the same way you'd notice the difference between a house with a few toys scattered around and one that's positively filthy. (Those of us who have raised kids tend to make analogies like that.)

Determine the Style of the Shop

The most important part of your visit is observing how technicians diagnose car problems. Remember my example of the doctor who suggested an appendectomy for a mild stomachache? The same holds true if a customer says, "A red light is flashing on the dash, and the battery goes dead," and the technician responds, "Yep, that's the alternator. The replacement will cost $200. Pay up front."

The technician couldn't possibly know what's causing that light to flash on your dash without first checking the car. The proper diagnostic steps for this problem would include checking the system for codes, checking the alternator output, and checking the alternator itself for a loose belt or loose connection. If someone skipped those diagnostic steps and instantly started yanking at components, I'd be inclined to think he's what I call a "parts replacer," that is, a technician who just keeps replacing part after part until by process of elimination he finds the faulty one. Sure, your car will eventually be fixed, but it's a pretty expensive way of doing it.

You also want to assess the technician or shop owner's willingness to communicate diagnostic methods, repair procedures, and estimated costs. If a tech is too impatient to explain your car's problem, he might also be too busy to repair the car properly.

A technician or service writer should answer questions or show you the work area. But don't just wander into a work area unescorted.

Estimates and Guarantees

One of the biggest tests will be determining the shop's method for estimating repair costs. You're probably in a good shop if they perform the correct diagnostic steps and then give you an estimated price range *before* they do any work on the car. Many times costs can't be completely calculated until the system is disassembled, but be wary of any shop that won't give you a worst-case-scenario price. If they won't give you a price *range*, then you shouldn't give them your business.

Finally, you'll want to know about a shop's guarantee policy, which tends to vary since very few states manage to regulate the auto repair industry. Some guarantees are for thirty days, others last a lifetime. Most major rebuilding jobs, such as transmissions or engines, usually carry one-year guarantees, but driver control affects certain systems—for instance, brake lining and manual transmission clutches—so it's harder to put a guarantee on those. Call a few shops to compare guarantee policies, and before any repair work gets under way, ask the shop manager these questions:

✔ How long is the repair guaranteed?

✔ Does the guarantee cover a certain time period or does it also have a mileage limit?

✔ Will a defective part be replaced or is it repaired as needed?

✔ Do you guarantee the repair you're making will fix the car's problem?

✔ Will I deal with this repair shop or the part manufacturer on the guarantee?

✔ Do I get the guarantee in writing?

Be aware that you'll have to return to the original shop to take advantage of most guaranteed work. Don't think you can have the work done elsewhere then take the bill back to the original shop to be reimbursed. It simply doesn't work that way, so it pays to choose a shop you're happy with in the first place.

A Quick Summary

Let's review the checklist for choosing a repair shop:

✔ Check with the Better Business Bureau or State Attorney General's Office for any complaints filed against a shop.

✔ Visit a shop for an informal inspection *before* your car develops problems.

✔ Evaluate the cleanliness and organization of a shop.

✔ Trust your feelings about a shop's personnel. Look for ASE certificates to verify skills.

✔ Ask about the shop's diagnostic process and how it determines a price range for repairs.

✔ Inquire about the shop's guarantee policies.

Now It's Your Turn

So let's say after all your hard work you've found the perfect shop. Now it's up to you to be a good customer. Keep your appointments and arrive on time. Pay bills promptly, and, if a problem arises, assume it was an honest error and return to the shop with the attitude that the problem can be resolved pleasantly. Give the techs a chance to check out the car instead of ranting or threatening them. Hysterical behavior will grant you instant persona non grata status in a shop, and you can say good-bye to any perks you'd get as a regular.

Having all maintenance and repair done at the same shop is good for your car because the technicians get to know its idiosyncrasies, and that can save time and money in the diagnostic process. But being a

Auto Advertising: The Old Bait and Switch

We've all seen the newspaper ads proclaiming "Complete brake job for $49.95!" or "Tune-ups for under $30!" You might go to this repair shop to take advantage of this incredible deal only to have the shop owner point out the fine print, which happens to say something like "Offer good on 1958 blue Edsels only."

Bait-and-switch advertising is a problem in any service industry, and car repair is no exception. Disreputable owners figure once you're in the shop, they've got you for better or worse, and they'll tell you that $49.95 really isn't for your type of car—yours requires more labor, more parts, and so on, and anyhow, the quote doesn't include cutting the drum brakes and rebuilding the calipers. In other words, it's not a *complete* brake job, after all. It's a sure bet the salesperson will then attempt to move you into another brake service for "just a few dollars more."

Impossibly low prices are just that: impossible. To prove it, let's examine the $49.95 claim. Brake lining for front and rear wheels will run you $30 to $40, and an hour's labor in most shops is between $30 and $50. Add a little overhead and the repair shop would actually lose money on a $49.95 brake job. No company survives if it's losing money on transactions, so what happens? If the shop stands behind the advertised price, it may make up the difference by using inferior parts or keep the price down by paying low wages to an unskilled worker. Either way, you lose.

loyal customer is good for you too because, as they say, membership has its benefits. A shop is more likely to cater to a regular customer, fix the annoying minor repairs, advise you on your car, even give you special attention in an emergency situation. Many times I've worked my favorite customers into a busy schedule or kept the shop open late just to accommodate them.

Everything Old Is New Again

Not every replacement part that goes into your car is brand new. That shouldn't alarm you because in some cases a brand-new part isn't necessarily the best one for the job. I run into customers all the time who refer to rebuilt parts as new, used parts as rebuilt, and in general experience a lot of confusion when it comes to this issue. New, rebuilt, and used parts all have their place in the auto repair industry, and each is ideal for certain applications. As the ultimate user of these parts, and the person who pays the bill, you should understand the distinctions.

New Auto Parts

New auto parts have been made either by the manufacturer of an automobile or they've been made to the specifications of the original part by an independent company. If the part was made by the car manufacturer, it's referred to as an original equipment manufacturer part, or OEM.

New parts made by independent companies vary widely in both price and quality. It's been my experience that many of them are equal to OEM quality, and in some cases they're less expensive. Conscientious shop owners are very selective about the suppliers of new parts because a defect can cause serious problems.

Rebuilt Parts

Rebuilt parts may also be referred to as reconditioned or remanufactured parts, but these terms all mean basically the same thing, and often they are the most realistic way to approach certain car problems. Re-built units are usually larger assemblies made up of many parts, such as transmissions, engines, or carburetors. You'll find many rebuilt parts boxed and stocked at parts stores. Water pumps, alternators, and starters are examples of parts that are almost always rebuilt units. Brake shoes and standard clutches are remanufactured by having new friction material applied.

Units to be rebuilt are disassembled, cleaned, and parts are replaced as necessary. A rebuilt transmission may cost you from $400 to $800, which is quite low compared to the $2,000 or higher cost of a totally new one. Rebuilt parts vary in price and quality, so you should also inquire about the brand of the part and details on the warranty. Sometimes warranties cover only the replacement of the part and not the labor to install it.

Used Parts

Used parts are salvaged from a vehicle similar to yours. They are usually supplied by an auto wrecker who buys wrecked or used vehicles to retrieve parts that are still usable. The parts might be cleaned before they go to the repair shop, but other than that they arrive as-is, which could be good or bad depending on the car they came from.

Most of these parts, regardless of cost, are guaranteed for thirty days, and on some occasions for ninety days. It's possible that a used part is the only one available for your car; if that's the case, request that the part be scrutinized carefully before installation.

As the car owner, not the repair expert, you probably aren't qualified to decide if a new, rebuilt, or used part is best for your car, but because of the differences in price and quality, the auto technician should discuss the possibilities with you and advise you on what he or she thinks is the best choice. (This is another good argument for why it pays to know and trust your repair shop.) If the tech doesn't bring up the issue of new, rebuilt, or used parts, then you should.

Gypsy Parts

There's another kind of auto part that you should be aware of: the "gypsy" part. That's how we in the industry refer to counterfeit car parts, and they come from all over the world. Their quality—or lack thereof—varies, but the price is often lower, and the boxes or labels frequently are designed to resemble brand-name products. In some cases the packages are actually fraudulent duplications. The auto industry isn't alone in fighting this influx of counterfeit products. The electronic, construction, clothing, and jewelry industries are all affected. After all, who hasn't seen at least one sidewalk vendor selling watches and jewelry with Rodeo Drive logos?

According to recent Federal Trade Commission statistics, auto parts counterfeiting is a $3 *billion* business annually in the United States, which means some repair shops may unwittingly or otherwise use counterfeit parts. This country manufactures many quality and well-known brands, so ask about the parts used at your shop. A good shop manager will be happy to share this information with you.

Respect Your Auto Technician

Here's my chance to get on a soapbox and extol the virtues of a good mechanic, uh, excuse me, I mean *auto technician*. (Sounds classier, don't you think?) I've been trying to teach you to respect the automobile for the miracle it is, but the auto techs are the people who keep that miracle on the road, so I think they deserve a lot of respect too.

Decades ago, the high school auto shop was a dumping ground for kids who couldn't cut it in academics. Today you can't work on a car unless you have extensive computer training, math skills, and superior analytical capabilities. Don't let a little grease under the fingernails fool you—the men and women working on your car go through considerable training, training that continues on a regular basis in order to keep up with the rapid technological advances in this industry. It already takes a two-year community college certificate and vocational-tech training to get an auto tech job, but I'm convinced that, with the continued technology, in another few years we'll be requiring four-year college degrees.

Automobile Association of America studies indicate a growing need for skilled auto technicians; already they pinpoint a shortage of more than 60,000 people. Anyone who owns a car should be concerned about that shortage, so do what you can to encourage bright young people to explore the field. According to AAA statistics, an experienced tech can earn between $25,000 to $75,000 annually.

Don't be shy about asking a shop manager to explain the technicians' training when you take a car in for service. You might be surprised to hear just how involved it is. And get to know the techs at a shop, get a feeling for their attitudes and personality. Skill and training are one thing, but combine it with natural aptitude and you've got a sure winner. One of my mechanics started out as a high school part-timer. He'd sweep up the shop, run errands, that kind of thing, and one day he asked me if he could have an old alternator lying around on a bench. I asked him what he wanted to do with it, and he told me that he and his brother were devising a method to generate electricity for their stereo using an automotive system. I gladly handed over the alternator and felt very thankful indeed that this kid worked for me. He's now twenty years old and one of the best technicians in my or any other shop.

"Methinks the Car Doth Pull Too Much" (or, Learning the Language of Mechanics)

All industries create their own private language, a certain way of speaking that identifies insiders and separates the amateurs from the pros. Eavesdrop on two auto technicians (or two stockbrokers, or two doctors, or two *anythings,* for that matter) and you might think aliens landed from another planet. It pays for you, the customer, to learn some of the language from the Land of Mechanics, because it just might help in the diagnosis of your car's problem. For instance, did you realize describing the engine as "hot" or "cold" has nothing to do with the weather outside? Understanding the vocabulary can translate into a more efficient repair for the tech and a lower repair bill for you.

Lazy   Lacking power, a car that "can't get out of its own way."

Slip   Engine revs, but the car doesn't move.

Hesitation or delay   Time lapse between putting the car in gear, or stepping on the gas pedal, and getting a reaction.

Hot   Temperature after the car is warmed up and running.

Cold   Temperature after the car has been sitting.

High-gear start   Transmission doesn't go back into first gear at a stop and takes off in high.

Acceleration   Stepping on gas pedal.

Deceleration   Still moving, but your foot is off the gas pedal.

Brake pull   Car pulls to one side when brake is applied.

Steering pull   Car pulls to one side as you steer.

Upshift   When transmission goes from low gear to high gear.

Downshift   When transmission goes from high gear to low gear.

Chatter   A condition that causes the car to feel like it's on a rumble strip.

Locking up   Car won't move; it feels as if it's against a brick wall instead of in neutral.

Coast down   Allowing the car to slow down to a stop by removing your foot from the gas but not using the brake.

Cranking   When the starter is turning but the engine won't start.

Taking your car to a new repair shop and trusting it to new auto technicians is a lot like being the new guy at work. You really have to get the lay of the land and get used to your new coworkers' personalities before you're completely at ease. Once you've been around for a while, you'll know just what makes the place tick and how you fit into the picture.

We Won't Be Undersold:

Buying a Car

I'm going to make a big leap here, from buying car parts to actually buying the whole car. It just seems like a good way to wind down because, after all, this whole milieu of maintenance and car care starts with your first car purchase.

Scan the shelves in a bookstore or even the magazine racks at the grocers and you'll find plenty of opinions about the right and wrong way to buy a car, and I'm not about to try to compete with that. What I *am* going to offer is my advice on how to choose the car that's right for you.

Admit it: Isn't there at least one ratty old pair of blue jeans in your wardrobe you absolutely love? They might have grass stains, holes in the knees, and tatters at the seams, but you've owned them *forever,* and the instant you put them on you feel happy and safe and comfortable. Or maybe it's the million-year-old armchair in your living room, losing its stuffing and faded with age, and hopelessly out of place among your more fashionable furniture. But you couldn't bear to part with it because anytime life gets tough you curl up and relax, knowing it's you and your armchair against the world.

I think more people ought to form similar emotional attachments to their cars. I couldn't even begin to describe my attachment to my first car, a burgundy GTO. You should really like your car, and I mean *like* it, not just the design but the way it performs, the places it takes you, the freedom it offers, and even if it starts to show signs of age, you ought to stick by it the way you would an old pal. Ask around. I'm sure you'll find at least one friend who names his or her car. And I've seen more than one shed some tears when it came time to trade in a favorite old vehicle—some of them so brokenhearted you'd think they were taking the beloved family pet to the vet to be put down.

I'm not suggesting you get overly sentimental—although I wouldn't discourage it either! I once had a customer so emotionally attached to her car that she actually "visited" it every day it was in the shop for repairs.

Plain and simple, I just want to see you respect your car. If you do you're more likely to maintain it properly and drive it carefully, and in return the car gives you a longer, safer lifetime of service. Buy a car that doesn't fit your needs or your lifestyle, drains your finances, or is inconvenient to service, and you can bet you'll build up a well of resentment toward it. The first step in forging a happy relationship with your vehicle is to buy the one that fits you just like that favorite pair of blue jeans.

The Basics Before You Buy

If you walk into a dealership and announce you're ready to buy, the first question you'll get is "What kind of car are you looking for?" If you answer, "A red one . . . with a really cool stereo," look out, because you are a car salesman's dream. It'd be easier to just walk into the dealership with a TAKE ADVANTAGE OF ME tag pinned to your shirt. You want a car that doesn't just look great but performs well, and since it's such a major investment, you'll have to do research—and lots of it. Start the research process long before you step inside a dealership, and put everything down on paper so you can refer to it during the buying process. Page 1 in this Car Buying Binder should address these critical points:

How Much Can I Spend?

✔ If you're financing a car, know how much you can put down out-of-pocket in case the value of your trade-in doesn't cover the down payment.

✔ Know what you can handle as a monthly payment, and figure in the monthly operating costs too (e.g., the cost of gas, the cost of maintenance, etc.). Nothing's guaranteed to cause resentment faster than a car that sucks up your whole paycheck.

What Are Your General Needs for a Car?

✔ Do you require a family car with lots of space? With lots of room in the trunk? Do you really want a convertible if you live in a city that gets rain four days a week? Will that sporty two-seater really serve you well if you have to chauffeur Grandma to the grocery store each weekend? Picture how the car fits into your real life, not the fantasy version of your life.

Where Do You Usually Drive the Car, and Where Do You Park It?

✔ Answering these questions tells you a lot about the kind of features to look for, whether it's four-wheel drive or a compact frame that can be squeezed into a tiny parking spot in the city. It also makes you think about the area in which you live. Luxurious or sporty vehicles could turn out to be crime magnets in a big city. Are you prepared to put up with that kind of hassle and worry?

How Flexible Are You about the Car You Want?

✔ Do you demand a racy little sports car because it projects a certain image? Do you insist on a big, heavy boat of a car because you're terrified of collisions? Will you drive only sky-blue cars with pink interiors? These factors affect how tough you'll be when it's time to negotiate price, so be honest with yourself about whether your decision is based on reason or if it's based on whimsy. One car-buying consultant I know, Mike Solito, tells his clients to live by the phrase "Never fall in love with anything that can't hug you back."

Decide If You Want to Buy Used or New

✔ Sometimes there's a big gap between the kind of car you *want* and the kind of car you can *afford,* so explore the possibility of purchasing a used car, particularly if you're in the market for something large or midsize. A car's largest depreciation in value occurs in its first three years. After that, depreciation slows, so if you find a four-year-old car that was really well maintained by its previous owner, you could be getting a better value than if you bought a new car.

Small or economy-size cars tend to wear out faster, so the depreciation rule isn't as true as it is for the big luxury models. If you're after something in this size range, you're better off buying new.

Buying Imports or American Cars

Many people, myself included, believe in buying American because of a personal philosophy, but what I'm talking about here has to do with purely practical factors in choosing between import and domestic cars.

During the 1980s, when some American cars had quality problems, all you ever heard was how much better the imports were. In the last decade, American engineering has become more innovative, styling is great, and quality is high. Manufacturers offer a wide selection, a variety of prices, and advanced service. On the other hand, imported cars have suffered in quality as they've gone into overdrive transmissions and more sophisticated electronic controls. Anyone who still believes imports are trouble-free should take a trip to my repair shop, where I regularly tally astounding repair bills on imports that had to wait long periods of time for parts. And yet American cars still fight a bad rep, just like the bad-news teenager who's trying to clean up his act but can't shake his old reputation.

The bottom line is you'll find good and not-so-good cars no matter where they're manufactured, so do your homework and base your selection on the car's performance—not its "nationality."

Does It Make Sense to Lease a Car Instead of Buy?

Leasing has become popular in the last few years, but it isn't the perfect choice for everyone. The main difference is that leasing is a partial purchase, paying only for the part of the car you use for the limited time that you use it. One leasing advantage is a lower down payment and lower monthly payments, but you still have to pay for all insurance, maintenance, and repairs on the lease. And you can't neglect maintenance just because you don't own the car; you'll pay a steep penalty at the end of the lease if the car is in poor condition.

To determine if a lease is right for you, consider these factors:

✔ How many miles do you put on a car each year? If the figure is high, don't consider leasing because at the end of the lease you're penalized for higher mileage.

✔ Do you like to keep a car long term? Most car leases are for two or three years, a good option for someone who likes to sport the newest model vehicle every few years. But if you're looking for a long relationship, stick with buying.

✔ You may have the option of buying the car at the end of the lease. In some situations the value of the car is much higher than the buy-out price, so you might want to purchase it yourself and then sell it to someone else in the hopes of making a profit. Just keep in mind that you might lose money that way too.

Let's Make a Deal

Once you answer these questions honestly, you can narrow down the field of choices. Then it's time to get out there and search for *where* you'll buy the car. You have to research the venues very carefully and choose from new car dealerships, independent used car dealers, or private owners. Some people find this process so intimidating or time-consuming that they invest a couple of hundred dollars to hire a car-buying consultant who will select a car for them and assist in negotiating price. (Check your local phone directory under "Car Buying Consultants" for a list of people who provide this service.)

For more information on selecting, negotiating price, warranties, road-testing, and taking delivery of a new car, flip through copies of *Consumer Reports,* go to the library or bank to check out the "blue book" value (just keep in mind those figures aren't carved in stone), or select any of the number of books devoted to the topic of car-buying. The selection is endless, the information extensive, and it would be irresponsible of me to try to sum it all up in just a few paragraphs.

The advice I would add to whatever research you uncover is *always* have your own auto technician evaluate a used car before you buy it, particularly if you're getting one from a private owner. You have very little recourse if you buy a problem car in a private sale, so be extremely cautious in your purchase.

If *you* are the person selling the car, insist that the buyer have it checked by a professional auto technician and then have a disclosure signed stating the condition of the car was established and that you have no further liability.

When the Honeymoon Is Over

O kay, so now let's figure you're at the *end* of the buying process, you get the car home, you take a long, hard look at it in your driveway, and you think, "Hmm . . . did I make the right choice? Did I really want a green car? Don't you think it's a little too sporty for my lifestyle after all?" Basically you're out of luck, because a car isn't like a new pair of shoes that can go back to the store if they pinch. The reason you take so much time and do such extensive research before buying is because you can't return a car just because you changed your mind.

But what happens if you buy a car and soon after it develops a major problem? Give the dealer the opportunity to take care of it. The next step would be to call the manufacturer's customer service department, and if all else fails, inquire at your State Attorney General's Office to see if your state recognizes a "lemon law," designed to force the dealer to buy back a new car that has severely malfunctioned.

Some states recognize a period of time after the purchase during which you may invalidate a sale. If a seller knew about a major defect on a used car but didn't disclose the information to you and sold it marked "as is," you may have grounds to cancel the sale. It's actually illegal to sell a car with a cracked engine block, so there's no trouble returning a car with that problem. If you think you've been misled or cheated, take your complaint to the Consumer Protection Agency or State Attorney General's Office and ask them to investigate.

When Teens Take a Turn Behind the Wheel

I might tell you to check *Consumer Reports* for your basic car purchase, but when it comes to the first car you purchase for your teenager, I have a lot more to say. This advice isn't coming from a "parent" (although after raising three kids, I've certainly done my share of car-shopping). This advice is coming to you from a career mechanic, and one who specializes in transmissions to boot. And nowhere will you see the damage from an overeager teen driver faster than in a transmission repair shop.

A few years ago a car was towed into my shop with the worst case of abuse I'd ever seen. The transmission was absolutely destroyed, and in ways that left no doubt about how it had happened. It looked like an explosion rocked the inside, and the sure cause of it was neutral drop. For those of you who haven't hung with the hot-rod crowd, "neutral drop" means revving up the engine to extremely high RPMs in neutral then throwing the car in gear.

Turns out the car was owned by a sixteen-year-old boy, and once I found out that detail, I was concerned about guaranteeing the work because this kid could go right back out and destroy his new transmission. When the teenager came into the shop to pick up his car, he was accompanied by his mother, a very nice widow trying to support her large family, and there she was stuck with a really high, unnecessary repair bill.

I saw my shot and I took it. I really lambasted this kid in front of his mother, told him he shouldn't be allowed to drive, that how he destroyed his transmission was a crime, and if the car ever came back with a problem I'd know exactly how he'd caused it. It must have sunk in because the car never returned—but a few years later this kid's mother called me. She said her second son was now learning how to drive, and she wanted to know if she could bring him into the shop for one of my lectures!

Actually, I'd hate to scare any teen who's just learning to drive, because getting your first car when you're that age is an important and exciting experience, and going into it with the right attitude sets a pattern that will last a lifetime. All kids should recognize the responsibility that goes along with a driver's license, and all parents should know about the kind of car that will make a teen's first driving experience safe. Here's a short list:

A teen's first car should teach:

✔ **Respect** for equipment. Proper care and maintenance will increase the life span of a big investment.

✔ **Responsibility.** Cars teach a very clear lesson about cause and effect. Drive like a cowboy and you'll use more gas; wear out tires, brakes, and the transmission faster; and speed the need for replacement parts.

✔ **Regard.** I really believe that first car should be part of a love affair. If your teen has regard for the car and is proud of it, you won't have to coax him or her to clean and wax it regularly.

A teen's first car should be safe:

✔ Buy a car that is big enough and heavy enough to offer more protection in a collision.

✔ The vehicle should handle easily. Many teens are attracted to the sporty appearance of sport-utility vehicles and vans, but they are more difficult to handle than conventional cars.

✔ A teen's first car should offer enough power for transportation, but not much more. (See sidebar, page 228.)

Your final consideration in buying your teen's first car is its cost. What can you afford? If you search carefully, you can find affordable solid cars, either new or used. Cross off any cars that come with expensive features, like a turbo-charge, because they cost a fortune to replace. Avoid gas hogs and exotic import cars where repairs will be costly. And never buy a car that some other car buff has "modified." They might look sharp, but often these cars are a nightmarish concoction of mismatched and impossible-to-replace parts. Modified cars rarely perform well, and if you're unlucky enough to suffer a breakdown, the odds for an easy repair are not in your favor.

Fun, Fun, Fun Till Daddy Takes My T-Bird Away

No new driver, especially a teen, should have access to a car with dangerously high horsepower. It's just too tempting to play Speed Racer in a car like that. When my first son turned sixteen, I was appalled at the cars he was eyeing, but then I realized, hey, the kid's been exposed to muscle cars, power, and speed all his life. After all, he grew up with a mother who was tearing around town in a GTO! Figuring I hadn't encouraged him to take the most conservative approach to cars, I finally parted with my beloved GTO and got a Buick sedan on which to teach him to drive. Sometimes you have to sacrifice "fun fun fun" for "safe safe safe."

Try to find a car the teen can maintain on his or her own. Kids will learn the most on that first car, so why discourage their efforts with a vehicle too complicated to service? I find the older (1970s and '80s) Pontiac Grand Prix and Olds Cutlasses make great first cars. They're simple but still very appealing in style, and they're solid enough to withstand a fender-bender.

Whether you purchase a car for the teen, or if the teen is now driving the family car, you can do a lot to teach responsibility to your new driver, including:

 Educate teens about cause and effect. Prove that good driving habits cost less than bad ones.

 Teach basic car care and small repairs. (This rule goes for the girls as well as the boys.) Don't let them take out the car until they can demonstrate certain tasks, for instance, how to change a tire or check basic fluid levels.

✔ Suggest teens pay for some or all of the maintenance and operating costs (e.g., fuel, car washes, insurance).

✔ Require teens to pay for any repairs caused by abuse. (That includes tire replacements.)

✔ Inform teens you will take away the keys to the car at the first sign of dangerous driving—and then make good on the threat if they challenge you.

If your teens are fast-approaching driving age, you have my encouragement—and my sympathies. Having raised three of my own, and seeing countless families come through my shop every day, I honestly can say you're in for a very interesting new chapter in your life as a parent.

But, hey, if I could give up my GTO, anything's possible.

Happy Trails to You

I have a confession: At this moment, I am just one point away from having my driver's license revoked for speeding. Speeding isn't something I do during peak traffic times. No, sir, *then* I am the model citizen.

But when no one else is around . . .

Maybe I should have been a Formula 1 racer instead of an auto technician, because there's a certain feeling that comes from being in control of a high-performance automobile, and sometimes it just possesses me. There was that morning in the mountains when I opened up the GTO and took some S-curves doing 120 mph. There were the occasional 2 A.M. drag races and even the innocent Sunday drives with my dog that got out of control. Give in to those temptations and sooner or later you're bound to bump into a state trooper who's less than thrilled with your antics.

I'm not saying all of this to impress you, like some teenager bragging about my dad's cool new car. I'm an adult woman (no need to mention my age specifically, but let's just say it hovers around the speed limit) with a business and a family and some grandchildren, and most people say to look at me I'm the last person they'd ever suspect of being a car fanatic. Frankly, I can't explain it either. It just strikes me every time I stick a key in the ignition just what a miracle a moving car is—kind of the same way some people think it's a miracle every time a million-pound airplane gets off the ground and flies.

I know of a man who was so inspired by his Corvette that he actually requested to be buried in it, that's how much he loved his car. Maybe that's a little wacko even by my fanatic standards, but it still makes an interesting analogy about the fun being in the journey and life being one wild ride. I might be "waxing poetic" while everyone else is just "waxing the car," but so what; who says you can't be practical and passionate at the same time? That's exactly the point I've been trying to make throughout this entire book.

Car culture surrounds us in this country. We have car clubs and custom competitions, race car heroes and a torrent of romanticized advertising. We have Greased Lightning and the legend of James Dean, and I can't even count the number of movies and songs that glorify the automobile.

So yes, there is a very definite and undeniable fantasy we weave around our cars, what they say about our personalities and our level of success. If you believe all those car commercials, it's what they say about our sex appeal, what they say about our freedom, and what they say about independence. To my mind, caring for your car—maintaining it, repairing it, respecting it—makes that fantasy just a little more real.

I hope this book and its information have helped you to cultivate more of an appreciation for your car. I hope it helps you protect your investment, feel more at ease as you drive, and hang on to the confidence it takes to tackle whatever problems you face along the way.

Most of all, I wish you one of those indescribable moments behind the wheel, when the windows are open and the wind is blowing through your hair and the sun is shining on your face and the road ahead is wide open, and just when you think life couldn't possibly get any better, your very favorite song of all time starts playing on the radio.

Now, if you'll excuse me, I think I'll fire up the Buick and contemplate the miracle of the automobile while I drive off into the sunset.

Let's just hope there aren't any speed traps along the way.

Appendix

Advocates for Highway and Auto Safety
750 First Street NE
Suite 901
Washington, D.C. 20002
1-202-408-1711
(Offers consumer fact sheets; works with a variety of coalitions to promote highway and auto safety)

Automobile Consumer Action Panel (AUTOCAP)
write to: National Automobile Dealers Association
8400 West Park Drive
McLean, VA 22102
(Covers 15 foreign manufacturers, sponsored by 15,000 local dealers)

Automotive Service Industry Association (ASIA)
805 15th Street NW
Washington, D.C. 20005
1-202-408-9550
(Statistical information on car sales, repairs, etc.)

Auto Safety Hotline
National Highway Traffic Safety Administration
8 A.M. – 4 P.M. weekdays
1-800-424-9393 or
1-202-426-0123 (Washington, D.C.)
(Information about recalls, crash tests, etc.)

"Car Care & Car-Cover Secrets"
Free brochure
1-800-424-8000
(Provides car, van, and truck seat covers and fabrics)

Global Shopping Network
P.O. Box 350506
Ft. Lauderdale, FL 33335
9 A.M. – 5 P.M. weekdays
1-800-221-4001
(Pricing service providing reports that compare wholesale and retail
prices for cars and trucks)

Insurance Institute for Highway Safety
write to: Safer Cars
Box 1420,
Arlington, VA 22210
(Send self-addressed stamped envelope for consumer information
about car safety, shopping for a safer car, and other automotive
safety-related issues)

Motorists Assurance Program
808 17th Street NW
Suite 200
Washington, D.C. 20006
1-202-466-7050
(Consumer information about vehicle repair)

National Car Care Council
1 Grande Lake Drive
Port Clinton, PA 43452
1-419-734-5343
(Material available on all aspects of automotive safety, consumer advice, and industry-related information)

National Institute for Automotive Service Excellence
13505 Dulles Technology Drive
Hernodon, VA 22071-3415
1-701-713-3800
(An institute that provides training and voluntary testing of automotive technicians and is a source of automotive service information for the automotive industry and general public)

SAV-A-LIFE Industries LTD
P.O. Box 1226
New York, NY 10025
1-800-654-3337
(1-800-OK-4-DEER)
(Free catalogs available, featuring daytime running lights, deer alert, doze alert, sleep warning devices, and other automotive safety devices)

Tire Industry Safety Council
P.O. Box 3147
Medina, OH 44258
(Send self-addressed stamped business envelope for free tire publications: *Motorist's Tire Care and Safety Guide* and *Recreational Vehicle Tire Care and Safety Guide* covering tire care, repair, and buying guide, etc.)

Glossary

A

Accelerator–Pedal to control the increase in a car's speed, commonly called the gas pedal.

Air filter–A filter designed to prevent dust and other particles from getting into the engine through the fuel system.

Alignment–Geometric setting of the front wheels to provide easier steering and optimum tire wear.

All-wheel drive–Similar in performance to a four-wheel-drive vehicle, an all-wheel-drive vehicle has a small unit bolted inside the transmission pan, or on the side of the transmission, to send power to all of the wheels.

Alternator–Car's electrical power source. When the engine is running, the alternator generates electricity to charge the battery, and supplies current to the car's electrical system.

Alternator belt–The belt connected at the crankshaft pulley that drives the alternator, which is the car's source of electrical power.

Antifreeze–Part of the coolant mixture. A 50–50 mix of antifreeze and water prevents freezing in winter and overheating in summer. Antifreeze also contains rust and corrosion inhibitors.

Antilock brake system–Modern braking system with computers to control each wheel individually to pump the brakes in emergency situations, stabilizing the car and in most situations reducing the stopping distance.

Automatic transmission–Hydraulically operated transmission that determines what gear the car should be in and shifts to that gear.

Axle–The shaft on which a wheel turns. In rear-wheel-drive automobiles it is a solid shaft; on front-wheel drives, CV (constant velocity) joints on each end allow flexibility.

B

Battery–A device for storing energy that provides current for the starter and operates lights and accessories when the engine is not running.

Battery terminals–Located on either the top or the side of the battery, terminals are the external electrical connections of the battery. Batteries have one negative terminal and one positive terminal.

Bearings–Used between two moving parts to prevent friction. They may use balls or rollers, and are always packed with grease.

Blue book–The official wholesale used-car guide, published once a week by the National Automotive Dealer Association.

Boots–Accordion-pleated rubber covers that retain grease in the CV joints on front-wheel-drive axles.

Brake fluid–Fluid used to operate the hydraulic brake system.

Brake shoes–A metal piece, shaped like an arc, with a veneer of friction material used in drum brakes.

Brake system–The combination hydraulic and mechanical system that stops the car. The brake pedal forces brake fluid (by means of a master cylinder) to hydraulic parts in each wheel, which in turn force friction material parts against the rotor or drum.

C

Caliper–Hydraulic device in disc brakes used to exert force on the brake pads, which stop the car by holding the rotor.

Camber–The outward tilt of the top of the front wheels, which is an alignment adjustment that prevents tire wear.

Carbon monoxide–Colorless, odorless, and poisonous gas produced by a car's exhaust system.

Carburetor–Component of the engine in which gasoline and air are mixed to create gas vapor.

Caster–The backward tilt of the front wheels, which is the alignment adjustment that gives a straight-ahead steer.

Catalytic converter–Part of the emissions system where unburned gas vapor is chemically changed to further cut down discharge of pollutants from the tailpipe.

Charging system–System that generates electricity for the needs of the car, using an engine-driven belt to operate an alternator.

Chassis–Frame and working parts on which the body is mounted.

Chock–A triangular-shaped block of wood or rubber designed to wedge beneath a tire to prevent slipping or rolling during a tire change.

Choke butterfly–Lid on top of the carburetor that controls the amount of air entering the carburetor.

Coil springs–Parts in the suspension system that help soften bumps absorbed by shock absorbers, and aid in keeping the car level.

Combustion–The burning of gas vapor which takes place in the combustion chamber.

Compression ratio–Ratio referring to the extent that the gas vapor is compressed in the cylinder. The more compressed the gas vapor, the more power it will produce when ignited.

Connecting rods–Rods that connect the pistons to the crankshaft.

Constant velocity joints–Joints on each end of front-wheel-drive-vehicle axles that provide flexibility. Also called CV joints, they are covered by black, accordionlike boots to retain lubrication.

Coolant–A 50–50 water-antifreeze mixture used in the cooling system that lowers the freezing point in winter and raises the boiling point in summer. Also a rust inhibitor.

Cooling system–System that circulates the coolant throughout the engine, flowing through water jackets around the cylinders to prevent overheating.

Crankcase–The housing for the crankshaft and its surrounding parts with a reservoir for the engine oil used to lubricate the engine.

Crankshaft–Large, heavy, strangely shaped shaft turned by pistons (attached by connecting rods) to produce torque (the power that moves the car).

Cylinders–Combustion chambers where ignition takes place.

D

Decelerate–To remove your foot from the gas pedal (accelerator).

Dieseling–Occurs when engine continues to run after engine has been turned off. Called "dieseling" because the engine is operating like a diesel engine, in which firing takes place without an electrical spark.

Dipstick–Measuring stick used for checking various fluid levels.

Disc brakes–A brake system that uses pads, lined with friction material, applied by a caliper to stop the wheel by grabbing the rotor or disc.

Distributor–Device for distributing electricity to the spark plugs of the engine.

Driveshaft–Shaft that connects the transmission in a rear-wheel-drive vehicle to the rear axle assembly. Has at least two universal joints for flexibility.

Drum brakes–A brake system that hydraulically forces brake shoes against the surface of a brake drum to stop the car.

E

Electrical system–System includes lights and accessories, the battery, starting circuit, charging circuit, and the ignition system.

Emergency brake–Brake that holds the car when parked. It is *not* designed for emergency situations.

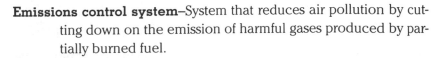

Emissions control system–System that reduces air pollution by cutting down on the emission of harmful gases produced by partially burned fuel.

Engine–In an automobile, the sole source of power, produced by the internal combustion of gas vapor.

Engine block–Heavy metal block in which the cylinders (combustion chambers) are located.

Exhaust gas recirculation valve–A valve in the emissions control system that works to further reduce air pollution.

Exhaust system–System by which exhaust gases produced by the combustion are removed from the engine and expelled at the rear of the car.

External transmission cooler–A second cooler through which the transmission fluid is run to dissipate heat further after it has gone through the cooler in the radiator. Advisable for vehicles that are heavily loaded or used to tow.

F

Fan–Operated by a belt connected to the crankshaft, the fan (located between the engine and radiator) draws air through the radiator, aiding the cooling system.

Fan belt–Belt that turns the fan, driven by the crankshaft.

Feeler gauge–Tool used to gap spark plugs to specifications.

Final drive–The rear end of a front-wheel-drive vehicle. It may be located inside the same case with the transmission or bolted to the side of the transmission. Axles fit into it and carry the torque on to the front wheels.

Firewall–The vertical metal panel that separates the engine area from the passenger compartment. The dash is mounted to it on the inside of the car.

Flywheel–Heavy plate with a gear attached that bolts to the rear of the crankshaft. The gear on the starter meshes with and turns the flywheel, which then turns the crankshaft and starts the car.

Four-wheel drive–System by which engine power (adapted in the transmission) is carried to both the front and rear wheels.

Front-wheel drive–Vehicle designed so that the engine torque is carried to the front wheels. The car operates with the front wheels pulling the car, as opposed to the rear wheels pushing the car.

Fuel filter–Filter in the fuel system that removes any foreign particles as the liquid gasoline flows through it.

Fuel-injection system–A system using sensors and other sophisticated equipment to enrich or thin the gas-air mixture and direct it to the combustion chamber. Used instead of a carburetor, fuel-injection systems are much more efficient.

Fuel system–Responsible for storing fuel, transporting it to the combustion area, and turning liquid gasoline into gas vapor.

G

Gap–The process of adjusting the space on the hooklike electrode of the spark plug's firing side.

Generator–The apparatus in early-model cars for producing electricity. In later-model cars this task is performed by the alternator.

Ground–Completes an electrical circuit and makes it possible for the current to flow.

H

Heater core–Small radiatorlike piece that the heated coolant flows through to the heater.

Heater hoses–Hoses that carry coolant to and from the heater core.

Hose clamps–Clamps that hold hoses stable.

Hubcaps–Caps that cover the ends of the wheel spindles. They protect the wheel bearings from salt and water and may be very decorative.

Hydraulic–Power source by fluid under pressure.

Hydroplaning–Dangerous driving incident that occurs at high speeds when water gets between the tire and the surface of the road.

I

Idiot lights–Lighting system on a car's dash that may flash red or display printed messages to warn drivers of impending problems.

Idle–Fuel system feeds just enough fuel for the engine to run when there is no load on it.

Ignition system–Means by which a high-voltage spark is produced and delivered to each spark plug, which then ignites gas vapor in the combustion chamber.

Intake manifold–Series of passages through which gas vapor goes into the combustion chamber. On fuel-injection systems some of the mixing of gasoline and air may take place in the intake manifold.

Internal combustion engine–An engine that produces power by burning a gas vapor inside the cylinders. The expansion of the burning gases forces the pistons down, turning the crankshaft and producing torque.

J

Jack–Device used to lift the car or a portion of the car off the ground to offer access to the wheels or undercarriage.

Jack stands–Stands on which a car can safely remain in a lifted position, for continued access to the wheels or undercarriage.

Jumper cables–Two separate heavy wires with alligator clips on the ends, used to conduct energy from a charged battery to a dead one.

K

Knock–Sometimes referred to as "spark knock," this noise is caused by an engine combustion problem.

L

Leaf springs–Parts in the suspension system that keep the car level and help soften bumps absorbed by shock absorbers.

Limp mode–System designed to prevent total failure of sophisticated, electronically controlled cars. Fuel and timing are no longer controlled by the computer, the engine runs but with very little power, and the transmission will usually stay in second gear, or, sometimes, third, allowing a car enough power to travel a short distance for servicing.

Lube job–Service intended to lubricate moving parts and systems on a car mostly around the front end. Later-model cars have many closed systems that require no lubrication.

Lug nuts–Small nuts designed to hold the wheel in place on the car.

Lug wrench–Tool designed to loosen and tighten lug nuts.

M

Manual transmission–Also called a *standard transmission*. A car's driver decides which gear to be in and then uses the clutch to physically move one gear to mesh with another.

Master cylinder–Mechanism that stores brake fluid and forces it to the four wheels to stop the car when the brake pedal is pushed down.

Mounts–Steel brackets with rubber cushions fused on to hold engine and transmission stable and to prevent vibration.

Muffler–The exhaust gases traveling from the catalytic converter end up in the muffler. This part muffles the roar of the engine, and the gases continues to pass into the tailpipe and out the rear of the car.

N

Negative terminal–Terminal on the battery that is connected to the ground. It will be marked with a "–" or *Neg* and is usually black in color.

O

Octane–The measurement of a gasoline's resistance to detonation or "pinging."

OEM–Abbreviation for "original equipment manufacturer." Describes a part manufactured and supplied by the manufacturer of the vehicle.

Oil filter–Filter through which engine oil flows. Impurities are removed from the oil and remain in the filter, which should be changed periodically.

Oil pump–Pump located in the crankcase that pumps oil to the moving parts of the engine.

Overdrive–A transmission design in which the output speed of the transmission is greater than the input speed, putting less demand on the engine and increasing fuel economy.

Overhaul–To disassemble a mechanism, clean and examine all parts, and replace all worn parts. Ideally the mechanism is restored to like-new quality.

P

Parking brake–Brake designed to hold the car when parked. An assembly in the car can be activated to pull brakes on in the rear wheels by means of cables.

Parking pawl–Small hooklike part in an automatic transmission that holds a gear so the car cannot move when the lever is placed in the park position.

Passing gear–In an automatic transmission, passing gear is activated by stepping down on the gas pedal while cruising in order to downshift the transmission to a lower gear, thereby gaining power to pass another car.

Petcock–Small faucet at the bottom of the radiator used to drain coolant.

Piston–Engine part forced into motion by expanding gas vapor, which then, by way of connecting rods, turns the crankshaft.

Positive crankcase ventilation valve–A valve in the exhaust systems of cars that works to further reduce air pollution from a car's emissions.

Positive terminal–Battery terminal that connects to the starting circuit and electrical system. Will be marked "+" for *Pos*, is usually red, and is often larger than the negative terminal.

Power booster–Power-brake system's vacuum-operated unit.

Power brakes–Brakes assisted by a vacuum-operated power booster to aid in braking.

Power steering–Optional feature that uses hydraulic force to assist a driver in steering a car.

Power train–Name given to the engine, transmission, driveshaft, and rear axle assembly. These components carry power from one end of the car to the other.

Pressure cap–The pressurized, removable lid of the radiator, raises the boiling point of the coolant proportionally so the system can run hotter without boiling over.

R

Rack and pinion–Lighter, more compact steering system that has re-placed the old-style gear box.

Radiator–Tank where hot coolant from the engine is cooled. Made up of a series of small tubes that carry the hot coolant through a honeycomb design where air blows through.

Radiator hoses–Hoses, one upper and one lower, that carry coolant to the radiator to be cooled and circulated back to the engine.

Ratchet–Tool that allows a socket or screw to turn one way and then, by moving a lever, turn in the other direction without having to remove the tool.

Rear axle assembly–The rear end of a car; where the engine torque changes direction from straight back, making a 90-degree turn and continuing to the axles and rear wheels.

Resonator–A small, auxiliary muffler usually found on luxury vehicles.

Rocker arms–Arclike mechanisms that are part of the system that opens and closes the valves in the engine. Found under the valve covers.

Rotor–The disc attached to each wheel in disc brakes. On top of each one is a caliper that grabs the rotor with pads lined with friction material and stops it each time the brakes are applied.

$\mathcal{S}$

Serpentine belt–One belt used in place of several, the serpentine belt snakes over several pulleys driving various systems.

Shock absorbers–Located near each wheel, these parts control the springs in the suspension system by allowing one bounce, and then absorbing the shock so the car can return to its normal level.

Spark plug–Issues an electrical spark to ignite gas vapor in the combustion chamber.

Spark plug wires–Heavy ignition wires that carry the ignition spark from the distributor to the spark plug.

Speedometer–Device that indicates a vehicle's rate of speed. Measurement is usually picked up at the transmission.

Starter–Round, cylinderlike electrical motor with a gear on the end that meshes with the flywheel gear, to turn the crankshaft and start the car.

Starting circuit–System that starts the car. Includes the ignition switch, battery, neutral safety switch of the transmission, and the starter.

Steering linkage–A series of arms, levers, and joints that allow the front wheels to move in the direction determined by the steering wheel.

Steering system–Means by which the car is steered. Includes the steering wheel, linkage, and front wheels.

Struts–Part of the suspension system, similar to shock absorbers but with coil springs built into the assembly.

Suspension system–Includes shock absorbers or struts, springs, and steering linkage to provide a smoother, shock-free ride for the passenger. It absorbs and controls car's bouncing action on rough roads.

T

Tailpipe–Pipe discharging exhaust gases behind the muffler; extends out at the bottom rear of the car.

Thermostat–Instrument for maintaining desired temperature in a car's cooling system.

Timing–The working together of the valves and ignition system—along with other parts of the engine—to get the electrical spark to the spark plug at precisely the right time for efficient engine operation.

Torque–Another word to describe power, could also be defined as "twist force."

Torque converter–Part that connects the automatic transmission to the engine and works with the transmission, using common fluid.

Transaxle–A power train device used only on front-wheel-drive vehicles that has both the transmission and final drive in the same case.

Transmission–A system of gears for transmitting engine power and adapting it to road and load conditions.

Tread wear indicators–Horizontal bars molded into tires to show when tread is wearing thin.

Trickle charger–Small battery charger that can be attached to the battery to charge a few amps per hour, enough to prevent a drained battery due to frigid weather.

U

Undercarriage–Term used to refer to everything underneath the car.

Universal joints–Parts at each end of the driveshaft that provide flexibility.

V

Vacuum–Force created by the absence of air, vacuum is used to operate many systems in the car. Can be very powerful, as in a cyclone.

Valve–Mushroom-shaped part on stem that opens and closes to allow fuel vapor in and exhaust gases out of the combustion chambers.

Valve cover–Rectangular pans that bolt to the engine block covering the rocker arms of the valve system.

Valve lifter–Parts used in the engine's valve system to open and close valves by means of hydraulic power.

Vapor–Substance in a gaseous state, such as gasoline mixed with air.

Viscosity–Refers to an oil's tendency to flow. Measured by a system developed by the Society of Automotive Engineers.

Voltage regulator–Part that controls the alternator, telling it when to produce more energy and when to produce less energy.

W

Water pump–Pump at the front of the engine, operated by a belt that circulates coolant throughout the radiator and engine.

Wear bars–Smooth, bare strips running horizontally, built into tires to indicate tread wear.

Wheel balance–The procedure of strategically placing weights on a tire to counteract extra weight on that tire and prevent front-end shimmy.

Wheel bearing–The antifriction connection that allows the front wheels to turn without wearing parts. Consists of balls or rollers submerged in heavy grease.

Wheel cylinder–Hydraulic part that forces the brake shoe against the drum in drum brakes.

Index

Entries in *italics* refer to illustrations.

A

ABS (antilock) brakes, 35–36, 198
Acceleration, 216
Additives, 70–71
Air bags, 135
Air conditioner, 13; and gas mileage, 189; leaks, 187; and overheating, 118
Air filter, *24*, 25–26; changing, 80, *81*, 144; checking, 48; lid, 25; problems, 170–71
Alignment problems, 150, 165, *165*; vs. wheel balance, 151
Alloy wheels, 108
All-wheel-drive, 15, *15*
Alternator, 12, 16, 20, 22–23; adjustment nut, 72, *73*; belts, 100; pivot bolt, 72, *73*; problems, 197; rebuilt, 213
Antifreeze, 94; and car storage, 101; dangers, 55, 182; flushing, 62–64; frozen, 122–23; leaks, 181–82; rusty, 182; seasonal check, 100; tester, 43, 94
Automatic transmission, 16; and gas mileage, 191; leaks, 183–84; problems, 147–50, 171
Auto technician: language, 216–17; skills, 214–15

B

Backfire, 172
Battery, 18–20; and car storage, 101; checking, 48; cleaning terminals, 43, 48, 55–56, 167; dangers, 54; dead, 139–41; jumping, 112–17, *116*; maintaining, 97; replacing, 57, *58*; terminals, 20, *20*, 113–15, *116*, 139; water levels, 140
Battery cable terminal puller, 43, 56

Bearings, dry or worn, 177
Belts: checking, 50, 99–100; problems, 166–67; replacing, 72–74, *73*; serpentine, 72
"Blue book," 224
Brake(s), 29–36; checking, 51; failure, 33, 123–24, 154; fluid leak, 153, 185–87; lining, *31*, 33, 154; maintaining, 33, 154; noises, 179; overheating, 158, 159; pads, 32, *34*; pedal, 30, 153–54; problems, 153–55; pull, 216; shoes, 30, *31*, *34*; in snow, 129; warning lights, 197–98
Burning odor, 156–57
Burns, avoiding, 54

C

Caliper, 30–33, *32*
Carbon monoxide, 27, 160, 176
Carburetor, 24–26, *24*, *89*, 131; cleaner, 141; and flooded engine, 120; rebuilt, 213; and smoke, 171
Car Care Binder, 42, 51
Car(s): buying, 219–24; buying, for teenager, 225–29; handling emergencies, 103–36; leasing, 223–24; maintaining, 80–95; maintenance checklists, 41–52; new "lemon," 225; selling, 224–25; small repairs, 55–78; storing, 100–101; systems of, 12–40; troubleshooting, 137–99; understanding, 7–9; washing, 52
Caster adjustment, 152
Catalytic converter, 28, *28–29*; odor, 157; plugged, 145
Cellular phone, 112
Center link, *37*
"Charge" light, 197

O

Octane, 176, 192
Oil-Dry compound, 186
Original equipment manufacturer
(OEM), 212

P

Paint: checking, 44; repairing, 77
Park, getting stuck in, 149–50
Parking brake, 34–35, *34*; dragging, 190; won't work, 154–55
Parking pawl, 150
Parts: gypsy, 214; new, 212; rebuilt, 212–13; used, 213
Parts company repair shops, 204
Petcock, 64, *65*
Pets, 134
Piston: brake, *32*; engine, 11–12; shock absorber, 39; strut, 40
Pitman arm, *37*
Points, 144
Positive crankcase ventilation (PCV) valve, 28, *85*; replacing, 76–77, *76*
Power booster, 35
Power brakes, 35; problems, 154; and stalling, 124
Power steering, 38; changing fluid, 65–66, *66*; checking fluid, 50–51; leak, 150, 174, 184–85; pump, 16, 38, *66*; and stalling, 124
Power train, 12–17, *13*

Q

Quick-service shops, 204

R

Rack and pinion steering, 152
Radiator: burns, 54; cap removal, 61–62; checking, 49; cleaning, 97, 98; flushing, 62–64, *65*; hoses, checking, 49–50; hoses, replacing, 67–69, *68*; and overheating, 119; sealing leaks, 69
Rain, 128
Rapping, 175
Rattle, 175–76
Rear axle assembly (rear end), 12, *13*, 14, 17; grease leak, 185; hum, 177
Rear-wheel-drive: power train, 13–17; transmission, 91, 184
Repairs: attempting, 53–55; dangers, 54–55; estimates and guarantees,

209–10; small do-it-yourself, 55–78; scheduling needed, 51.
Repair shops, 201–17; being good customer, 210–12; choosing, 206–9; estimates and guarantees, 209–10; and parts, 212–14; sales tactics, 206, 211; technicians, 214–17; types, 202–5
Reservoir tube, 39
Resonator, *28*, 29
Return spring, *31*
Road and load conditions, 13
Road test checklist, 51
Roaring, 176
Rocker arms, 172
Rod problems, 175
Rotor, 30, *32*, 33, *34*; replacing, 144
"Rotten egg" odor, 157
Rubber mallet, 43

S

Safety: and antifreeze, 182; and carbon monoxide, 160; driving, 134–36; and gas leaks, 156; guidelines, 105–6; and packing, 132–33; in rain and snow, 128–30; and repairs, 54–55; and teenager drivers, 228–29; and trailer, 133–34
Seamless eye ring, 39
Seat belts, 135
Serpentine belts, 72
Service group (SF), 87
Shell: shock absorber, 39; strut, 40
Sherman, Ruth, 3
Shimmy, 151
Shock absorbers, 38–39, *39*; checking, 45; problems, 152–53, 168; and tire wear, 166, *166*
Singing, humming or howling, 177, 185
Skids, 128, 129
Slip, 216
Smoke, 170–71
Snow, 128–31
Solito, Mike, 222
Sounds, 172–80
Spare tire or donut, 46; and flats, 107, 111–12; rotating, 96
Spark plugs, 8, 11, 16; and car storage, 101; and flooded engine, 120; and ignition system, 23; replacing, 58–61, *60*; socket, 43; and tune-up, 144; wires, and electrical shock, 54; wires, replacing, 58, 61
Specialty repair shops, 203
Speedometer, 194, *195*
Springs, 40

Lucille Treganowan was born in Kansas and studied at the University of Arizona in Tucson, where she met her first husband and moved to his hometown of Pittsburgh. Too embarrassed to move back to Kansas with her three small children when her marriage failed, she pursued a career in the only thing she knew: auto repair. She opened her first shop, Transmissions by Lucille, in 1973 and now operates two shops in Pittsburgh, employing nearly thirty people. Her weekly half-hour television show, "Lucille's Car Care Clinic," can be seen throughout the country on HGTV and in Pittsburgh on WQED-TV.

Gina Catanzarite is the producer of "Lucille's Car Care Clinic" and a writer/producer at WQED Pittsburgh, where she has worked for the past four years producing special projects and talk shows. A journalist and award-winning poet and screenwriter, Catanzarite holds bachelor's degrees in nonfiction English writing, film theory, and American Sign Language for the deaf. She was born in Pittsburgh, where she still resides.